CURRENT AFFAIRS

Decision Making in a Nuclear Middle East

Lessons from the Cold War

Ozzie Paez

DECISIONS TO LEAD / FORT COLLINS, CO

Ozzie Paez
Fort Collins, Colorado
www.ozziepaezresearch.com

Book Layout © 2014 BookDesignTemplates.com
CreateSpace Publisher

Decision Making in a Nuclear Middle East - Lessons from the Cold War
Ozzie Paez. -- 1st edition.
ISBN 978-1532837579

To Ella Wolfe and Thomas Sowell for inspiring my own journey of discovery!

Since wars begin in the minds of men, it is in the minds of men that peace must be constructed.

—UNESCO CONSTITUTION

CONTENTS

{ i }

Preface

Some beliefs seem so logical that we take them for granted, only to be surprised when they later prove false. For example, many believe that the United States and Soviet Union never seriously considered starting a nuclear war or proliferating nuclear weapons because they recognized the risks and horrors of nuclear Armageddon. Official records declassified after the Cold War show that at least one of the superpowers did, in fact, consider a preemptive nuclear war, while the other made plans to transfer tactical nukes to revolutionaries with little governing experience. The same records reveal that the superpowers planned and actively prepared to use nuclear weapons in multiple occasions. If you are among the many, including academics and policy makers, who believe that the Cold War turned out as it was destined and that history suggests a similar outcome for a nuclear Middle East, then this book should give you pause.

The Unexpected Peace

We lived in the shadow of nuclear Armageddon for over forty years. And if you lived, as I did, near missile fields and major command centers, then you knew that the start of nuclear war likely signaled the end of your life, family and community. If the missiles went up, you'd have thirty-five minutes or less to live, with nothing to do but hug your kids and those you loved, provided they were close enough to reach in time.

Then, unexpectedly, the Cold War came to an end, the Soviet empire collapsed, democracy spread across Central and Eastern Europe, and the superpowers' focus shifted from building bigger and better nukes to reducing their nuclear arsenals. Communist China also evolved, becoming less communist and more capitalist, viewing America less as a mortal enemy and more as both competitor and customer of its growing industrial-manufacturing economy.

A few hotspots remained: in Asia, where nuclear-armed India and Pakistan were still at odds, and on the Korean Peninsula, home to North Korea's unpredictable leadership. We continued to worry, of course, but the remaining threats were generally known, contained and remote. Those countries didn't threaten the world, just each other. And there was hope that new generations, growing up free of the Cold War and in a more inclusive age, would reverse course and do away with their nations' nuclear arsenals.

Precedents existed in South Africa's 1993 decision to voluntarily relinquish its nuclear weapons, end its nuclear weapons program and sign the Treaty on the Non-Proliferation of Nuclear Weapons (NPT); and in the decision by Ukraine, as a new nation following the collapse of the Soviet Union, to shut down its part of the Soviet nuclear weapons complex and give up the nuclear stockpile on its territory.

A Reversal of Fortunes

As unlikely as it once seemed, by the turn of the century it increasingly felt like the age of nuclear weapons was quietly coming to an end. Maybe the nuclear genie could be put back in the bottle after all! Then the pendulum reversed with the Iranian government's increasing determination to join the nuclear club. As with most big decisions, this one was a process, not an event, but the Supreme Leader and Mullahs who lead the Islamic Republic concluded that it was in their nation's best interest to develop nuclear weapons and the missiles to deliver them to enemies near and far. The nuclear genie was back in business and this time in one of the most historically violent, yet economically important regions of the world.

There was hope, for a while, that the major nuclear and economic powers would act in unison to force a change in

Iranian policy and prevent a new nuclear standoff. The presumption by many was that this was an issue former Cold War adversaries could, should and would agree on. As it turned out, the Russian and Chinese governments, after initially voting in favor of sanctions, eventually came to see a nuclear Iran more as a valued commercial customer than a threat to world peace.

They are not alone in their views; a small but influential contingent of Western scholars and policy makers have portrayed an Iran–Israeli nuclear standoff as analogous to the Cold War. They believe, based largely on Cold War outcomes, that the risks created by a nuclear-armed Iran would be manageable and that a new balance of power in the region might lead to greater stability and peace. After all, they reasoned, the Cold War led to nearly fifty years of peace in a previously violent European continent and made it possible for new political forces to emerge that were generally peaceful, economically successful and largely democratic.

The most prominent proponent of this view was the late Kenneth N. Waltz, senior research scholar at the Saltzman Institute of War and Peace Studies and adjunct professor of political science at Columbia University. Writing in *Foreign Affairs*, Waltz pointed out that there are few options outside of military force to prevent a country from becoming a nuclear power:

> *...the historical record indicates that a country bent on acquiring nuclear weapons can rarely be dissuaded from doing so.... If Tehran determines*

that its security depends on possessing nuclear weapons, sanctions are unlikely to change its mind.[1]

He then made the case for proliferating nuclear weapons based on the assertion that they deter reckless behaviors and promote peaceful coexistence between nuclear adversaries:

...Despite a widespread belief to the contrary, Iranian policy is made not by "mad mullahs" but by perfectly sane ayatollahs who want to survive just like any other leaders. Although Iran's leaders indulge in inflammatory and hateful rhetoric, they show no propensity for self-destruction....

If Iran goes nuclear, Israel and Iran will deter each other, as nuclear powers always have. There has never been a full-scale war between two nuclear-armed states....

Most important, policymakers and citizens in the Arab world, Europe, Israel, and the United States should take comfort from the fact that history has shown that where nuclear capabilities emerge, so, too, does stability. When it comes to nuclear weapons, now as ever, more may be better.[2]

Waltz's views may not be mainstream, but they have been influential and provide intellectual cover for those who don't see an existential threat to Israel in a nuclear Iran. They have also found a receptive audience among foreign policy experts who believe that Iran will never voluntarily give up its quest for nuclear weapons, leaving a dangerous and destabilizing military option as the only alternative for preventing it. In this context, an Israeli–Iranian nuclear standoff and coexistence is the more attractive, logical option. These views and their implications will be tested in the chapters ahead.

Decision Making in Nuclear Environments

The central idea of this book is that to understand the risks of a future nuclear standoff between Iran and Israel—and to apply practical lessons from the Cold War—we must first understand the similarities and differences in the two decision-making environments. Speculating about the future based on how the Cold War turned out is not enough, particularly since our interpretations are often distorted by the damaging bias of hindsight.

The analytical approach of this book focuses on the judgments and decisions of American and Soviet leaders and policy makers during the Cold War. It considers their strategies, policies, actions and reactions during dangerous incidents and major events such as the Cuban Missile Crisis. This line of research only became possible after large volumes of documents were declassified and made available following the collapse of the Soviet Union and the end of the Cold War. They enabled us to witness Cold War history through the eyes of decision makers facing the threat of nuclear war on both sides and to understand their decisions in light of what they knew and did not know at the time.

This view of history is detailed and operational, and sheds light on how real human beings made judgments under high uncertainty with the fate of their nations and millions of lives in the balance. It reveals the strengths and weaknesses of their decisions, and offers new insights into their personalities, influences and tolerance for risk. Rather than subsuming the humanity of the Cold War into generalized outcomes, it places human beings at the center of the drama, with their abilities and liabilities in play.

Drilling into momentous Cold War events and crises opens windows into the behavior of veteran politicians, diplomats, policy makers and military leaders who had lived through World War II, the most destructive war in human history. They had witnessed the carnage of that war and the first use of nuclear weapons. For them, the violent killing of millions was no abstraction. By considering their decisions in the context of their experiences, times and environment, and taking into account the potential of an Israeli–Iranian nuclear standoff, the following questions emerged to guide the development of this book:

- Were the outcomes of the Cold War largely predictable because of the deterrent effects of nuclear weapons and nuclear war? Did nuclear weapons promote thoughtful, rational decisions by the superpowers? Did the superpowers avoid taking unnecessary risks that could lead to general nuclear war?

- How analogous is the environment of the Middle East to that of the Cold War? What options did the superpowers consider for addressing mounting tensions, threats and shifts in the balance of power? Are those options practical in a Middle East operational environment? What lessons emerged from the first two decades of the Cold War that can help decision makers today assess the risks of a nuclear standoff in the Middle East?

- Which lessons learned from operational, systems and human failures during the Cold War would be applicable to a nuclear Middle East?

- Are there structural differences between Iran and Israel that give either side advantages the other could not practically overcome? Are these differences sufficient to create existential threats by and for either country or both?

These questions kept the focus on the practical, operational, human side of nuclear weapons control, management and use. These considerations are often lost in abstract discussions over visions, philosophies and global forecasts by diplomats, policy makers and political leaders. They are always present, however, when the unexpected happens, a crisis emerges and the threat of war suddenly looms. Given the stakes of nuclear conflict, we ignore them at our peril.

A Roadmap

The book is organized into three general parts. The first three chapters cover the history of the nuclear age from just after World War II through the Cuban Missile Crisis. For the United States, it involves the administrations of Harry Truman, Dwight Eisenhower and John Kennedy, while the Soviets were led by Joseph Stalin and Nikita Khrushchev. Other leaders of this period that figured into the background investigation included British Prime Ministers Clement Attlee, Sir Winston Churchill, Anthony Eden and Harold McMillan, French President Charles de Gaulle and Cuban dictator Fidel Castro.

Chapters four and five consider the technologies, human factors and structural environment of the Middle East and their implications for a potential nuclear conflict between Iran and Israel. They examine Iran's stated strategy for destroying Israel and the potential for further proliferation of nuclear weapons in the region. The final two chapters discuss lessons from the Cold War, analyze Iranian nuclear weapons as an existential threat to the State of Israel and consider the implications for a potential nuclear war in the region.

I have included an extensive list of references from varied sources that can help readers explore the ideas, events and history behind this book. There will also be discussions and future papers available on my website at http://ozziepaez research.com. I encourage you to join the conversation. Of all the issues our world is facing, none has the potential to affect more people than a nuclear conflict, particularly in a region so critical to the world economy and the faiths of billions of people.

{ 1 }

After the War

The Cold War is the best case we have to shed light on the many challenges, risks and uncertainties of a future nuclear Middle East. While the two environments are distinctly different, the Soviet–American nuclear standoff has many lessons to offer if we look beyond hypothetical generalizations and simple analogies. Nuclear weapons in the aftermath of World War II were initially no more controversial than other highly destructive technologies and tactics used during the war. Understanding their implications for military and political strategy, developing effective controls and managing the vast resources needed to design, test and produce them proved much more difficult.

Possessing nuclear weapons had systemic effects on national security, the economy, foreign policy and other areas of statecraft than the Americans and Soviets initially assumed.

11

Over half a century ago, some of the best minds in science, economics, war and politics struggled to understand the implications of going nuclear. We now realize that they frequently fell short and in the process sometimes brought the world closer to nuclear war than they intended. Similar challenges, risks and uncertainties will face new generations should the Middle East host a contemporary, even less predictable version of the Cold War.

This chapter focuses on the assumptions, struggles and decisions of leaders, policy makers and military strategists of the early nuclear age as they considered if, when and how nuclear weapons could and should be used. They worked tirelessly to make sense of operational environments changed by nuclear weapons and worried about the implications for the security of their nations. Their experiences, decisions and resulting outcomes may help today's leaders to better understand the risks and uncertainties of a nuclear Middle East. In the balance will be the world economy, the future history of the Holy Land and the lives of millions of people across and beyond the region.

The Quantum Leap

Nuclear weapons were introduced as a quantum leap in military technology with an almost unimaginable capacity for destruction. Their distinctive advantage was in the power to quickly and efficiently deliver massive damage to the enemy, which during World War II had required waves of bombers flying dangerous missions over multiple days to drop thousands of tons of high explosives and incendiaries. For example, in one of the most horrific conventional bombing campaigns of the War,[3] which took place in February 1945, over 1,000 RAF and US Eighth Air Force bombers dropped 3,900 tons (3.9 kilotons) of high explosives and incendiaries on the ancient German city of Dresden. Between 35,000 and 100,000 people, mostly civilians, are estimated to have died in the ensuing firestorms.[4]

By contrast, on Monday, August 6, 1945, a single B-36 bomber, the Enola Gay, dropped one 15-kiloton atomic bomb on Hiroshima that obliterated everything in a one-mile radius, instantly killing over 90,000 people. An additional 40,000 to 80,000 would die over the coming years from radiation exposure and burns.[5] Three days later, another B-36 dropped a more powerful 20-kiloton nuclear bomb on Nagasaki that instantly killed over 80,000 people and injured tens of thousands more.

The shock delivered by just two nuclear bombs prompted Emperor Hirohito to accept Allied terms of surrender five days later on August 14, 1945. In his radio address the next day, the Emperor acknowledged the role that nuclear weapons had played in his decision:

> *The war situation has developed not necessarily to Japan's advantage, while the general trends of the world have all turned against her interests.... The enemy, moreover, has begun to employ a new most cruel bomb, the power of which to do damage is*

*indeed incalculable... [it is] according to the
dictates of time and fate that we come by enduring
the unendurable and suffering what is insufferable.*[6]

Even these relatively small nuclear weapons demonstrated man's new capacity to lay waste to entire societies in relatively short periods of time. The two bombs also saved the Allies the unenviable task of invading the Japanese islands at a projected cost of one million (primarily American) casualties and an equal number of Japanese military and civilian deaths.

The bombings suggested that nuclear weapons could replace expensive conventional forces in many campaigns by delivering mass destruction quickly and cheaply. The expected savings from replacing conventional forces with nuclear weapons appealed to the Truman administration, which had come under pressure immediately after the war to demobilize American forces and reduce defense spending. American families wanted their boys home and protests were breaking out at home and in military bases overseas by draftees demanding to be sent home before their two-year enlistments were up.[7] Congress responded by reducing defense budgets and decreasing manpower ceilings for all branches of the military.

The results were deeper cuts in Army and Navy strength between 1946 and 1950 than the services recommended. The Army, for example, had planned for peacetime ground and air forces levels of 1.5 million men. The Navy called for 600,000 men, 370 combat ships, 5,000 other ships and 8,000 aircraft.

Their requests turned out to be wishful thinking. By June 1947, the Army had been reduced to a volunteer body of 990,000 men, including 306,000 airmen, representing less than one-eighth its peak during the war.[8] The Navy was reduced to 498,000 officers and enlisted[9] or approximately one-seventh of its 3,405,525 peak on July 31, 1945.[10] These reductions deeply impacted operational readiness due to the loss of experienced service personnel, and lead to widespread deterioration of military equipment. New trainees were poor replacements for experienced combat veterans.[11] Still, the Truman administration felt secure in the knowledge that the United States was and would remain the sole nuclear power for years to come, and that nuclear deterrence would keep troublemakers in check. Those assumptions were soon tested by former allies turned adversaries.

A Problematic Alliance

The alliance between the United States, Britain and the Soviet Union had centered on a common enemy, Nazi Germany. The allies held two important conferences on developing common post-war policies and fostering cooperation. The first one, at Yalta in the Crimea from February 4 to 11, 1945, was attended by Joseph Stalin, Prime Minister Winston Churchill and President Franklin Roosevelt. Divisions quickly emerged during the conference between Stalin and the Western Allies over the future of Central and Eastern European nations, and their right to democratic self-determination.

The second, held at Potsdam from July 17 to August 2, 1945, was attended by the new US President, Harry S. Truman, who took a harder line with the Soviets on democratic self-determination. He tried to pressure Stalin to comply with the spirit of Yalta by hinting that America would soon have revolutionary weapons of enormous power, but Stalin, whose spies had already informed him of America's nuclear bombs, was unmoved.

Truman's tougher line with the Soviets was translated into a coherent strategy the following year by George Kennan, a diplomat, scholar and Soviet observer then stationed at the US embassy in Moscow. Kennan recognized the need to check Soviet expansionism without resorting to another devastating European war. He outlined his ideas for Secretary of State George Marshall in a communique dubbed "the long telegraph," where he detailed a long-term Soviet containment strategy. He cautioned against using ruthless methods to counter Stalin's aggressive policies, pointing out that "the greatest danger that can befall us in coping with this problem of Soviet Communism, is that we shall allow ourselves to become like those with whom we are coping."[12]

Kennan was then reassigned to Washington where he made a public case for a containment strategy in an anonymous essay published in *Foreign Affairs* titled "The Sources of Soviet Conduct," by Author X. He asserted that "it is clear that the United States cannot expect in the foreseeable future to enjoy political intimacy with the Soviet regime. It must continue to regard the Soviet Union as a rival, not a partner, in the political arena...."[13] Kennan's ideas helped shape Truman's foreign policy and remained influential for decades.

The End of the Alliance

It was against this backdrop that Truman delivered a speech on March 27, 1947, before a joint session of Congress in which he argued that the United States had to assist free peoples in their struggles against totalitarian regimes because allowing totalitarianism to spread would "undermine the foundations of international peace and hence the security of the United States."[14] It came with a request for $400 million to help Turkey and Greece beat back internal and external communist threats. Weeks later, on June 5, 1947, Secretary of State Marshall delivered his famous address to the Harvard University graduating class, laying out a plan to help Western European countries rebuild their economies through unprecedented levels of American economic aid.

The Marshall Plan ran into initial opposition in Congress over its price tag but was ultimately saved by Stalin's brutal policy of forcing communist governments on the countries his armies occupied. All remaining Congressional doubts evaporated after the Soviet Army camped just outside Czech borders to make sure that a communist-led government took over on February 25, 1948. Then, on March 10, the uncooperative, pro-Western former Foreign Minister Jan Masaryk was "suicided" by the communists.[15] These events, which reminded many Americans of Hitler's aggressive actions ten years earlier, prompted Congress to approve the Marshall Plan, which pumped over $13 billion into Western European economies.

Aggressive communist moves over the next twelve months "sealed the deal" for American post-war foreign and military policies. In June 1948, the Soviets blockaded Berlin, triggering a faceoff between the former allies and the Berlin Airlift, which supplied the beleaguered city by air. By the time the blockade ended in May 1949, Western Europe and the United States had negotiated and signed the North Atlantic Treaty Organization (NATO), which was ratified by the US Senate in July of that year. The most important component of the Treaty was Article 5, which committed all NATO member states to consider an attack on one to be an attack on all.

NATO formally extended America's nuclear umbrella and security commitments to Western Europe, an unprecedented policy for the United States at the time; traditional American isolationism died when NATO was born. Then, on August 29, 1949, the Soviets exploded their first atomic bomb, and soon after, on October 1, Mao Zedong proclaimed the formation of Communist China. To many American and Western leaders, it seemed clear that communism was on the march.

The Cold War Takes Hold

The Truman administration was suddenly dealing with a very different world as the United States became formally entangled politically, economically and militarily in Europe and Asia. America needed a new national security policy and Truman formed an interagency group to craft it, in light of deteriorating relations with Moscow and new threats from communist China. Their recommendations came in a 58-page report, NSC-68, "United States Objectives and Programs for National Security," which was presented to the National Security Council on April 14, 1950.

NSC-68 considered a number of alternatives before recommending "the rapid building up of the political, economic, and military strength of the free world" as the most practical option.[16] Its recommendations shaped American security policy in the remaining years of the Truman administration, led to the tripling of defense spending as a percentage of GDP and increased taxes to pay for it.

Truman's expectations that America's nuclear arsenal would deter communist aggression didn't materialize. NSC-68 acknowledged it and effectively ended post-war plans for deep reductions in military spending. Stalin had called Truman's bluff in Berlin and the President blinked when he realized that the nuclear option was the only option. In practice, his thinking of nukes as just more powerful weapons of war had started to change almost as soon as he had proposed relying on them to cut defense spending. The change was reflected in his decision to keep nuclear weapons under civilian control, as he explained on July 24, 1948: "As President of the United States, I regard the continued control of all aspects of the atomic energy program, including

19

research, development, and the custody of atomic weapons, as the proper functions of the civil authorities."[17]

As the horrific aftermaths of Hiroshima and Nagasaki were revealed, Truman became increasingly introspective about the use of nuclear weapons and their impacts on civilian populations:

> *I don't think we ought to use this thing unless we absolutely have to. It is a terrible thing to order the use of something that is so terribly destructive... this isn't a military weapon. It is used to wipe out women and children and unarmed people and not for military uses. So we have to treat this differently from rifles and cannon and ordinary things like that.*[18]

Unfortunately, his defense priorities and budgets didn't evolve with his thinking, leaving the country with a diminished conventional military—and nuclear weapons he wasn't willing to use. Then, on June 25, 1950, North Korea invaded South Korea with the assistance and encouragement of the Soviet Union and Communist China. American military forces in South Korea were unprepared to engage a determined enemy with seemingly little fear of nuclear weapons. The United States won an important diplomatic victory at the United Nations by pushing a resolution authorizing the use of force to repel North Korean aggression, but conventional ground forces in South Korea initially struggled to stop the communist onslaught.[19]

The Korean War was the first time since Nagasaki where an American president had the opportunity to use nuclear weapons against a blatant act of aggression. But Truman refused requests from field commanders, including General Douglas McArthur, to put nuclear weapons at their disposal. He opted instead to reinstitute the draft and rely on conventional forces to fight a costly, protracted war, while relegating nuclear weapons to backing up diplomatic initiatives.

From Truman to Ike

At the end of 1952, the Korean War was still in progress and the US was facing mounting threats from the Soviet Union and Communist China, including their active support for North Korea's continuing war against the South and UN Forces. There was good news on America's national security front, however, as the production of nuclear weapons increased and the nuclear stockpile grew to about 800 bombs. Conventional forces were stronger and defense spending had significantly increased. The next President would have to update national security policies to address growing Soviet nuclear capabilities.

Dwight D. Eisenhower was easily elected in 1952 and took office the following January. With him came John Foster Dulles, an influential lawyer and diplomat with an interesting history, to serve as his Secretary of State. Dulles proposed a new approach to stem communist expansionism, which he outlined in "A Policy of Boldness," published in the May 19, 1952, issue of *Life* magazine, where he asserted:

There is one solution and only one [to secure free nations]: that is for the free world to develop the will and organize the means to retaliate instantly against open aggression by Red armies, so that, if it occurred anywhere, we could and would strike back where it hurts, by means of our choosing.[20]

Surprisingly, Dulles had been a peace activist before, during and immediately after World War II, writing eloquently about the horrors of war in general and of nuclear weapons in particular. He had advocated putting nuclear weapons under the control of international organizations, co-authoring a statement advising that, "…as soon as practicable control of this cosmic power be placed under international supervision at [the] service of peace and human welfare."[21] It was the spread of "godless communism" and the Berlin crisis that changed his views on war, nuclear weapons and their role in preserving democracy and American values.

Eisenhower—who had served as Supreme Allied Commander during the war, and then Chief of Staff of the US Army and Supreme Allied Commander in Europe—brought a new multidimensional view of security and national power to the presidency. Military strength, in his view, had to be balanced against economic, social and institutional health. He rejected Truman's costly buildup of conventional and nuclear forces, along with related tax increases and high defense spending. His views were reflected in the "Restatement of Basic National Security Policy," NSC 153/1, published on June 10, 1953, six months after he was sworn into office:

A vital factor in the long-term survival of the free world is the maintenance by the United States of a sound, strong economy. Efforts to build up free world strength rapidly have resulted in a high rate of Federal spending in excess of Federal income, at a time of heavy taxation. Continuation of this course of action over a long period of time would place the United States in danger of seriously weakening its economy and destroying the values and institutions which it is seeking to maintain....[22]

Eisenhower feared that the US would face both economic and military challenges in the standoff with the Soviets: "The basic problem facing the United States is to strike a proper balance between the risks arising from these two threats."[23] His revamped strategy (called "The New Look") relied on the threat of massive nuclear retaliation to deter communist threats to the United States and its allies. Costs were to be contained by reducing spending on conventional forces.

Changing of the Guard in Moscow

Joseph Stalin died in March 1953, leaving four senior party officials in charge of the Soviet Union: Georgi Malenkov, Lavrenti Beria, Vyacheslav Molotov and Nikita Khrushchev.[24] Beria, Stalin's last brutal henchman and head of the feared secret police, or KGB, was considered a threat by the others, who had him arrested in July 1953, then secretly tried and executed on December 24 of the same year.[25] The ensuing power struggle was settled within a year as Khrushchev elbowed the others aside to become the undisputed leader of the Soviet Union.

Khrushchev proved to be a tough, crafty adversary who could charm one moment and threaten global nuclear war the next. In general, when he saw an opportunity for advantage, he took it; when he suspected weakness in an opponent, he moved to test it. He had a penchant for unpredictability and brinksmanship that made him a difficult and particularly dangerous character in the developing Cold War drama. For American presidents and other Western leaders, dealing with Khrushchev's personality became a recurrent exercise in judgment under high uncertainty.

Eisenhower's Strategy

Nuclear weapons, like most revolutionary weapons technologies, became operational before political and military leaders fully understood their political, tactical and strategic implications. They were initially considered more powerful, less expensive munitions capable of replacing conventional bombing and artillery. Truman initially agreed with these views, but came to see nuclear weapons as too destructive for general battlefield use. Eisenhower reexamined Truman's strategy and made changes to align the use of nuclear weapons with his updated national security policy.

The Korean War was the type of long, bloody, costly struggle that Eisenhower was determined to avoid, even if it meant using nuclear weapons. Korea was the first test of his policy, and he reportedly warned the Soviets and Chinese that the war had to end or he would authorize the use of nuclear weapons. The pace of negotiations quickened in the months that followed, leading to the signing of an armistice agreement on July 27, 1953. The administration's New Look strategy seemed to work as Eisenhower and Dulles had envisioned. The new national security policy shifted resources from conventional forces to expand the nation's nuclear capabilities. No other president during the Cold War added so many nuclear weapons and weapon systems to the American arsenal. And no other president so clearly threatened potential enemies with massive nuclear retaliation if they attacked the United States or threatened vital national interests.

America's adversaries knew that Eisenhower had allowed the mass bombings of enemy population centers during WWII, so his credibility was airtight. The problem would come later, when a young president without his experience, credentials or credibility occupied the White House. In the meantime, Eisenhower would face a variety of crises around the world, and his strategy of threatening massive nuclear retaliation would be repeatedly tested by Khrushchev and Mao.

Implications

Nuclear weapons did not reduce defense costs, as initially expected, and instead led to overall increases in defense spending. The United States and Soviet Union built large nuclear arsenals, which were primarily used to deter direct conflict between each other. They deterred the Soviets from pushing into West Berlin and Western Europe, and the Western allies from challenging Soviet control of Central and Eastern Europe.

Building and running a nuclear weapons industrial complex ultimately proved too expensive and technically challenging for most countries. Even the United States, with its intact post-war economy had to choose between focusing on an unmatched nuclear arsenal and an unmatched conventional military. The added costs of nuclear weapons programs forced a reduction in conventional military budgets, which in turn led to greater reliance on nuclear weapons.

By the early 1950s, the United States recognized that nuclear weapons were no panacea and could not be used indiscriminately. Nuclear powers needed the right strategy to effectively use them and, most importantly, to avoid having to use them. It took the US and Soviet Union many years to hone their nuclear strategies as the Cold War evolved. Their experiences suggest that nations involved in future nuclear standoffs will similarly face challenges in leveraging their nuclear arsenals in the pursuit of national interests, while avoiding actual conflict. This is a complex, multifaceted endeavor fraught with risks and high uncertainty with the fate of nations in the balance.

{ 2 }

Eisenhower's Crises

Truman and Eisenhower recognized that nuclear conflicts were fundamentally different from conventional wars. Both presidents were clear in their willingness to use nuclear weapons, but only under specific circumstances and with their personal authorization. The primary difference between Truman and Eisenhower lay in their willingness to invest in nuclear and conventional forces. Truman wanted the flexibility of using conventional forces in situations that did not involve Soviet aggression against the United States and its allies. Eisenhower concluded that the United States could not afford the permanently high defense spending required by Truman's policies, so he relied primarily on the threat of massive nuclear retaliation to deter the Soviets, communist Chinese and other adversaries. His policies, budgets and priorities favored nuclear over conventional capabilities.

The decisions Eisenhower made in the face of an increasingly dangerous Soviet Union help illuminate the choices Israel and its Sunni Arab neighbors will soon face if Iran, as generally expected, continues to pursue nuclear weapons. The question facing Israel and regional Sunni Arab states is whether at some point the Islamic Republic will become so threatening that they have to preemptively to put an end to its nuclear ambitions. On the other side, Iran has to play for time to establish its own nuclear deterrence before fully unleashing its regional ambitions.

There is Cold War precedence for preemption as a policy to prevent an adversary from becoming a nuclear power. In the 1950s, the Eisenhower administration considered a preemptive nuclear war with the Soviet Union to eliminate the mounting communist nuclear threat. The use of nuclear weapons was also considered in a number of other crises, like those discussed below.

From War to Precarious Peace

The Korean War ended in an uneasy truce on July 27, 1953. The Armistice Agreement was signed by General Mark W. Clark as United Nations Commander; Lieutenant General William Harrison, Jr., for the United Nations; and Lieutenant General Nam II for North Korea. South Korean Major General Choi Kuk Chin, a former member of the UN Armistice Team, attended and then boycotted the signing, which no South Korean representative endorsed. South

Korean President Syngman Rhee promised to observe the armistice "for a time" while a political solution to reunify the country was pursued.[26] The West may have been relieved, but they were hardly convinced that it would hold. General Clark released a message the same day pointing out the need for a political settlement: "I must tell you as emphatically as I can that this does not mean immediate or even early withdrawal from Korea. The conflict will not be over until the Governments concerned have reached a firm political settlement."

That sentiment was echoed by General Maxwell Taylor, Eighth Army commander in Korea: "There is no strong feeling that our problems here are over, nor that the armistice is an occasion for unrestrained rejoicing."[27] Their words have proved prophetic as a large contingent of US forces remains in Korea six decades later.

The Korean War validated for Eisenhower his view that the US must avoid long, costly, limited wars. The conflict settled nothing and left combatants glaring at each other across the same 38th parallel that separated them at the start. America had paid a terrible price in lives and treasure without achieving a clear victory. As reported by the *New York Times,* the United States "suffered a total of 139,272 casualties. This included 24,965 dead, 101,368 wounded, 2,938 captured, 8,476 missing and 1,525 previously reported captured or missing, but since returned to military control."[28] The cost to American taxpayers totaled $30 billion, or $300 billion today.[29] Evidence suggests that Eisenhower would not have committed additional blood and dollars and would not have accepted defeat. That left nuclear weapons as the means to end the war, if diplomacy failed.

Crisis in the Taiwan Straits—Round 1

On September 3, 1954, the Communist Chinese began an artillery bombardment of Quemoy Island in the Taiwan Straits, where the anti-communist Nationalist Chinese kept a garrison. Quemoy was one of a number of tiny islands claimed by Communist China and the Nationalist government of Formosa (Taiwan). The barrage killed many Nationalist soldiers and several American advisors. The United States was unclear as to the strategic value of the islands in question; even Formosa itself had originally been outside of America's defensive perimeter. Unfortunately, these issues would have to be clarified while attacks intensified over the following months, leading to shifting positions and policy proposals from the State Department and Military Joint Chiefs, along with Allied calls for restraint, particularly from the British government.

The Joint Chiefs quickly developed action plans per existing nuclear policy guidelines. These included the use of nuclear bombs to suppress shore batteries, with options for a sustained inland nuclear campaign. The CIA estimated that a nuclear campaign could kill between 12 and 14 million Chinese, depending on how deep into the country the bombing extended. Military planning proceeded under the assumption that the Communist Chinese were preparing to invade the islands with an estimated half a million troops and over 700 aircraft, including more than 400 jets. The Nationalist Chinese could not match the Communists in strength, and the Joint Chiefs determined that the only practical alternative for stopping the invasion was to use nuclear weapons against shore positions and expand the attacks inland if the Communists did not back down.

Eisenhower listened to input from the military and intelligence agencies. He consulted with his Secretary of State and discussed options with his British counterparts, who remained opposed to the use of nuclear weapons over a few tiny, relatively unimportant islands. While he did not give a green light to the use of nuclear weapons, the President used the nuclear threat to open channels to the Chinese government. In the meantime, increased air surveillance found no evidence of Communist preparations to invade the islands, which made it easier for the US to seek a negotiated diplomatic solution. It took six months to deescalate the crisis without resorting to nuclear weapons and the ensuing massive loss of life. The negotiated solution also avoided a potential escalation to global nuclear war with the Soviets, who were allied with China.

General Chiang Kai-shek, the Nationalist leader, was deeply disappointed and angry with Eisenhower over the decision to avoid war. He viewed the crisis as an opportunity for the United States to eliminate the Communist Chinese government, but that would have risked a wider war with the

Soviets and potentially many years of military entanglement in China. Eisenhower was determined to avoid long, costly, bloody entanglements and was unwilling to lead the US into a nuclear conflict over a few islands of minor strategic value. He was also careful to keep his thinking from the Communist Chinese, Soviets and even his close British allies.

Atomic diplomacy worked to America's advantage in this crisis because the Communists recognized (or were led to believe) that the US would resort to nuclear weapons to prevent defeat but would also negotiate to prevent war. The strategy paid off just as Eisenhower and Dulles had hoped when they crafted The New Look and its reliance on massive nuclear retaliation. The issue of Taiwan, Communist China, the tiny islands and US involvement had not been entirely settled, but the negotiation provided a lull to evaluate and fine-tune America's national security policy.

Taiwan and Communist China—Round 2

On August 23, 1958, the Chinese Communists began shelling Taiwanese military forces stationed on the Quemoy and Matsu Islands. It was American policy after the 1955 crisis to help Taiwan defend the tiny islands. Taken literally, this meant that a Chinese attack on the islands would trigger an American military response. Khrushchev had previously hinted that the Soviets had provided the Chinese with tactical nuclear weapons. It was a bluff, but in a nuclear context, such bluffs can have major consequences. In response, the United States threatened nuclear strikes against Chinese positions. The Joint Chiefs informed the President that stopping the Communists militarily meant using, at a minimum, low-yield nuclear weapons against shore positions. Notes from meetings, planning sessions and war preparations show that the military held few reservations in using nuclear weapons.[30] By existing policy, tactical nuclear weapons had been designated as alternatives to conventional munitions and were particularly useful, at least in theory, where the US lacked sufficient forces to repel an enemy attack. There were concerns, however, that a nuclear attack on Communist Chinese batteries might lead to nuclear retaliation against Taiwan and the US Seventh Fleet. Soviet involvement, which Khrushchev had threatened, could also escalate the crisis into a general nuclear war the US did not want.

The British government weighed in on the crisis, reiterating its fears that the US might resort to nuclear weapons to defend tiny islands with little military or strategic value. They were concerned about the reaction in Britain and within NATO, something Dulles expressed to Joint Chiefs Chairman General Nathan Twining while inquiring about a conventional alternative. Twining responded that their studies clearly identified the need to use nuclear weapons. The official report of the meeting remarks that "…he [Twining] could not understand the public horror at the idea of using nuclear weapons…" and that he believed "we must get used to the idea that such weapons had to be used."[31]

In the end, Eisenhower guided the process to another non-military resolution, which again infuriated his Nationalist ally, General Chiang Kai-shek. The resolution forced Chiang to remove the bulk of his forces from the islands, which officially remained part of Taiwan. The President once again succeeded in avoiding a conflict that, in his mind, could have escalated into general nuclear war. His solution pleased America's British ally, but others watched and wondered if American resolve might be weakening. Different frames of reference produce different interpretations of events, which can entice adversaries to behave recklessly.

Berlin 1958–59:
Risks, Uncertainties and Nuclear Perils

On November 10, just a few months after the crisis in the Taiwan Straits, Khrushchev pounced on what he'd perceived as a potential softening of America resolve. He gave a speech to a visiting Polish group in which he called for the end of the occupation of Berlin and unilaterally offered to return control of the Soviet sector to East Germany. He then recommended that the Western Powers (US, Britain and France) do the same.

Khrushchev's actions triggered a near-immediate response from his former allies, who rejected his unilateral proposal and warned him that they were willing to defend West Berlin with force. That, however, involved some wishful thinking by the Western Powers, given that Britain and France were reluctant to risk another European war. The United States had recently studied the situation in Berlin and developed a policy in case of Soviet mischief, NSC 5727 Supplement I, "Statement of Policy on US Policy on Berlin." The first bullet under General Considerations stated: "Under existing treaties and US policies, an attack on Berlin would involve the United States in war with the USSR."

In the event of another blockade, the document outlined a series of actions that the US hoped would force a change of course by the Soviets. Otherwise, there was a backup plan:

> *If Soviet harassment nonetheless continues to threaten Western access to Berlin, the security interests of the United States and its Allies will require them to take immediate and forceful action to counter the Soviet challenge, even though such countermeasures might lead to general war.*[32]

The paper was clear that these were risky policies for precarious times: "If either side miscalculates, the situation could grow into war, even though neither side desires it."

Once again, the American military prepared for a potential nuclear conflict, this time over a more important principle: Soviet coercion and the Western Powers' rights in Berlin. Khrushchev made it as difficult as possible for Eisenhower and the allies to negotiate by framing the crisis so that any agreement would seem like capitulation. On November 27, 1958, Soviet Foreign Minister Andrei Gromyko handed American Ambassador Llewellyn Thomson a note that was long, threatening and framed as an ultimatum. Khrushchev warned that:

> *Methods of blackmail and reckless threats of force will be least of all appropriate in solving such a problem as the Berlin question. Such methods... can only bring the situation to the danger point.... But only madmen can go to the length of unleashing another world war over the preservation of privileges of occupiers in West Berlin. If such madmen should really appear, there is no doubt that strait jackets could be found for them....* [33]

The tactic initially worked, as the British in particular showed grave concerns over a potential nuclear confrontation in Europe and pushed for meetings by the heads of state.

There were many in the US Department of Defense and State Department who wanted to call Khrushchev's bluff and embarrass him into backing down, but Eisenhower refused to go along. He would not approve contingency plans that could pin him down, opting for the flexibility to make adjustments as the crisis played out. This incremental, flexible decision-making strategy, which may appear indecisive, is frequently indispensable in situations where there is high uncertainty and a high cost of failure; nuclear war over Berlin qualified on both counts. In the end, Khrushchev didn't want to fight a war with a more powerful adversary and backed off from his ultimatum.

Why Didn't Eisenhower Go Nuclear?

The simple answer, at least from the American perspective, is that none of these crises, from Korea to Berlin, involved an immediate threat to a vital national interest of the United States. Eisenhower came closest to using nuclear weapons in Korea, where mounting costs in lives and treasury were becoming as unacceptable as surrender; the armistice made going nuclear unnecessary.

The small islands in the Taiwan Straits were symbolic in the struggle with communism but were not a vital American interest. Attacking the Chinese mainland with nuclear weapons would have been costly for America's reputation and for its relationship with key allies, particularly Britain. The President found a way to check communist aggression by threatening to do what he privately wanted to avoid: unleash America's nuclear arsenal.

Even Berlin was not strategically vital in Eisenhower's calculus. He had previously framed it as an indefensible outpost deep in enemy-controlled territory and as a dangerous irritant in the relationship with the Soviet Union. It was important psychologically, particularly to Berliners and West Germans, but Britain, France and other European governments did not want to risk a nuclear war over access to the city.

In all of these crises, there were risks of stumbling into an unwanted nuclear war, and that danger was often aggravated by Khrushchev's bluster, bluffs and unpredictability. At no point, however, was the United States faced with the choice of using nuclear weapons or losing in the field. And in every case, both sides had time to consider options, take incremental steps, adjust their positions and make compromises. Thankfully, they avoided irreversible, categorical decisions that would have left them with no choice but to escalate crisis into conflict, while viable negotiated options were still available.

Nevertheless, there were multiple points during each crisis where a misstep or communist threat might have convinced the President to unleash the Strategic Air Command on the Soviet Union, Communist China and their allies. In each case, the Joint Chiefs developed detailed plans to carry out a global nuclear campaign and several times moved SAC bombers into position to execute them. The possibility of nuclear war was never just bluffing and idle talk.

{ 3 }

Kennedy's Turn

In early 1960, my father was recruited by a CIA operative in Cuba who introduced him to one of Castro's couriers. The man showed him evidence that the Castro brothers were in contact with the Russians and that the Cuban Revolution was being hijacked by communist agitators. The operative then asked my dad if he was willing to join the anti-communist underground and fight for the democracy the revolution had promised.

My father was in a tough spot. If he reported the men to the authorities, they would be arrested, brutally interrogated and executed by firing squad (euphemistically termed *paredón*, after the "big wall" behind the condemned). If he said nothing and the government later discovered that he had kept quiet, then it would have been the *paredón* for him, as well. He had risked his life just by listening. He accepted the dangerous "job offer" and that night became an American intelligence asset on the island.

A Young President in the Hot Seat

President Kennedy was sworn into office in January 1961 and faced his first crisis just three and a half months later when a brigade of CIA-trained anti-communist Cubans landed at the Bay of Pigs on April 17, 1961. The operation had been planned during the Eisenhower administration and approved by Kennedy after taking office. It called for the brigade to move inland from the beaches, establish a new government and request American recognition. Internal support would come from the CIA-managed underground network and others on the island who opposed Castro's increasingly repressive policies.

The operation ran into problems from the start, and the plan to use the underground failed, as Castro's secret police quickly rounded up thousands of suspected members, including my father. Thankfully, he escaped the notorious *paredón*, where many of his friends and colleagues breathed their last. The invasion turned into an embarrassing fiasco for Kennedy and a propaganda victory for Castro. The Soviets watched, took Kennedy's measure and looked for opportunities to exploit what they saw as American indecisiveness.

Berlin—*Again*

Kennedy and Khrushchev met in Vienna in June 1961 to discuss a range of issues, including ongoing disagreements over Berlin. The President asserted that the US considered Berlin an important strategic issue and would not agree to turn it over to East Germany. While no final agreement was at hand, the US and its Western allies believed that a negotiated resolution of existing differences was possible. Those hopes faded when Khrushchev unexpectedly demanded the reunification of Germany on communist terms. Kennedy rejected the proposal, but some believe that, in the process, he unintentionally hinted at accepting the permanent division of the city.

The Soviets latched on to this "concession" and gave the East Germans the green light to seal off their sector of Berlin.[34] Tensions grew as the world press reported the unilateral actions of the Soviets and East Germans, and the muted response of the Western Powers. The President informed the American people of the situation in a July 25, 1961, televised speech to the nation. He stressed that America's position was to seek a satisfactory resolution, provided that the Soviets didn't resort to making unreasonable demands:

> *...If they have proposals—not demands—we shall hear them. If they seek genuine understanding—not concessions of our rights—we shall meet with them. We have previously indicated our readiness to remove any actual irritants in West Berlin, but the*

freedom of that city is not negotiable. We cannot negotiate with those who say "What's mine is mine and what's yours is negotiable."[35]

In early August, Khrushchev again threatened to sign a separate treaty with East Germany if the Western Powers did not agree to turn Berlin into an open city. Kennedy responded with Congressional requests for large increases in American military manpower, including 125,000 soldiers for the Army, 69,000 for the Air Force and 29,000 for the Navy.[36]

Closing the Gateway to Freedom

On August 12, 1961, the communists upped the ante when East Berlin Mayor Walter Ulbricht ordered his forces to seal the border between East and West Berlin with temporary barriers that would grow into the notorious Berlin Wall. The daily exodus of nearly 2,000 East German refugees suddenly came to a halt. The Soviet army moved three divisions closer to Berlin and, along with East German units, made a massive show of force. In response, Kennedy called up nearly 150,000 reservists and National Guardsmen.

Toward the end of summer and into the fall of 1961, East German and Soviet forces engaged in a campaign of harassment against Western forces traveling across East Berlin. On October 22, the US Chief of Mission in West Berlin was stopped by East German and Soviet soldiers while crossing Checkpoint Charlie on his way to a theater in East Berlin in his car, which displayed occupation forces license plates. In response, US General Lucius Clay, Special Advisor in West Berlin, decided to call the Soviet–East German bluff by meeting force with force. In "A Brief History of the Berlin Crisis of 1961," Neil Carmichael writes:

> *The next day, Clay sent an American diplomat to test the East German border police. When the diplomat was stopped by East German transport police asking to see his passport, waiting US Military Police at the border recognized his diplomatic car, and rushed to escort him into East Berlin. The shaken GDR police moved out of the way. The car continued on and the soldiers returned to West Berlin. Over the next three days American and Soviet soldiers deployed at Checkpoint Charlie tested each country's resolve on how far each would go during these standoffs over Berlin....*
>
> *On October 27, 1961, the provocative games took a serious turn as another probe prompted the Soviets to deploy 10 tanks on the Eastern side of Checkpoint Charlie. The US had been using tanks to support their escorts of vehicles into East Berlin, and now was met by equal force. The Soviet and American tanks stood a mere 100 yards apart from each other, and both sides readied for battle.... The confrontation made headlines around the world and it looked as if the Cold War was soon to become a hot, shooting war with grave consequences....[37]*

In this crisis, the Soviets enjoyed overwhelming superiority in conventional forces. The only American options would have been to respond with nuclear weapons or surrender West Berlin. The danger was that an outbreak of fighting or a miscalculation could have led to a nuclear conflict that neither side wanted. This is what nearly happened. Instead of managing the dispute and avoiding provocations, General Clay continued to challenge the Russians and East Germans without realizing that the US and Soviet governments were already working on a political deal to deescalate the crisis.[38] Poor communication and delayed awareness by both sides on the ground in Berlin allowed confrontations and risks to mount, even as the governments involved were finalizing agreements for resolving their differences.

Playing Eisenhower's Hand

Kennedy came to power with a national security strategy based on flexible response, an approach Eisenhower had explicitly rejected. As a result, America's military force structure was initially ill-suited to support Kennedy's approach for containing communism. For example, his new strategy required stronger conventional forces than were available when he took office. What's more, the country's nuclear forces had been structured to quickly escalate any limited exchange into a global war. Kennedy didn't like it, yet he had no choice but to stick with Eisenhower's strategy until his military leaders made the changes he wanted.

In the meantime, Kennedy was forced to rely on the threat of global nuclear war during the 1961 Berlin Crisis, just as Eisenhower had in 1958–59. Fortunately, Khrushchev was keenly aware that the Soviet Union had comparatively weak nuclear capabilities, and evidence suggests that he did not see a nuclear war as a practical means for achieving Soviet aims. He therefore agreed to a negotiated solution rather than risk a general war with the Americans. By this time, his attention was shifting to his next and most reckless gamble, which led to the most dangerous crisis of the nuclear age: the secret introduction of Soviet medium-range ballistic missiles onto the island of Cuba.

Cuba: The World on the Brink[39]

In early 1962, reports by CIA agents on the island and by refugees escaping to the US began to show a pattern of Soviet military activities around the municipality of San Cristobal, in the province of Pinar del Rio. New CIA director John McCone, an engineer and businessman who had previously served as head of the Atomic Energy Commission, became increasingly alarmed by the reports and by evidence of growing Soviet military arms shipments to the island, including advanced fighters, fighter bombers and surface-to-air missiles (SAMs). He tried to warn the White House, but the Agency had lost much credibility over the Bay of Pigs fiasco, and he failed to persuade the President to authorize expanded air surveillance.

McCone's remaining agents in Cuba, including my father, were tasked with looking for signs of suspicious Russian military activities. They reported an increase in the number of Soviet military personnel and technical advisors, including many in the area around the port city of Mariel. The Director continued to warn the White House and Defense Department, which did little in response until late September 1962.[40] It's ironic that when the CIA possessed the best information within the US government, it lacked the credibility and influence to have its warnings taken more seriously. The Administration's failure to heed them allowed the mounting threat to go undetected until it was almost too late.[41,42]

On October 14, American surveillance aircraft finally flew over areas of concern identified by the CIA, and photo analysts quickly found signs of missile site construction activities. Two days later, the President's National Security Advisor McGeorge Bundy informed him that there was "conclusive evidence that a Soviet missile base was under construction near San Cristobal...just 90 miles from the coast of Florida." US intelligence was also concerned that other hardware had been hidden in the area, where dense foliage and large, naturally occurring caves provided ideal cover. So, while analysts poured over photographs, the remaining men of the Cuban underground were instructed to observe and report signs of unusual military and construction activities, equipment transports, Soviet technical personnel and new off-limit areas.[43]

Kennedy initially responded by forming a small executive group within the White House, the ExCom, to quietly assess the threat, come up with options and offer recommendations. On October 18, Soviet Foreign Minister Andrei Gromyko visited the President, who, without revealing what he knew, warned him of grave consequences if the Soviet Union attempted to introduce offensive weapons into Cuba. Gromyko repeated Khrushchev's previous assurances that no such weapons would be shipped to the island. Kennedy was reportedly surprised and furious that Khrushchev and Gromyko would blatantly lie to his face. It would not be the last time his wily adversaries would take advantage of his and his administration's naiveté.

After reviewing available intelligence and considering a variety of options, the ExCom developed two alternatives: (1) an air attack followed by an invasion and (2) a naval blockade to quarantine the island and prevent further shipments of Soviet military hardware, including nuclear missile components. Kennedy listened to the arguments and settled on the blockade option. He was concerned that an American invasion might lead to a direct confrontation with the Soviets and potential nuclear war.

According to Soviet documents declassified after the end of the Cold War, by the start of the blockade Soviet forces already had dozens of tactical nuclear weapons available on the island. These included 80 warheads for land-based cruise missiles, twelve warheads for the Luna/Frog launcher and six nuclear bombs for IL-28 fighter-bomber aircraft. Questions remain over the authority of commanders to use tactical nuclear weapons against an American invading force, but documented discussions at the highest level of the Soviet government, the Presidium, suggest senior officials expected that tactical nuclear weapons would likely be used to repel an invasion. Interviews with surviving Soviet commanders that served in Cuba during the crisis indicate that they were prepared to use nuclear weapons. The Soviets and Cubans had no other practical option for countering American superiority so close to US shores.[44]

Searching for Face-Saving Compromises

On October 22, Kennedy briefed former Presidents Herbert Hoover, Harry Truman and Dwight Eisenhower; formed an Executive Committee within the National Security Council; and notified members of the cabinet and congressional leaders. He then wrote a short personal note to Nikita Khrushchev in which he noted:

> ... I have not assumed that you or any other sane man would, in this nuclear age, deliberately plunge the world into war which it is crystal clear no country could win and which could only result in catastrophic consequences to the whole world, including the aggressor.

The President's evening speech to the nation informed the American people that he had instructed American military forces to blockade and quarantine the island of Cuba, in order to stop the Soviets from installing nuclear missiles 90 miles from US shores. The speech delivered a clear warning to Khrushchev:

> *It shall be the policy of this Nation to regard any nuclear missile launched from Cuba against any nation in the Western Hemisphere as an attack by the Soviet Union on the United States, requiring a full retaliatory response upon the Soviet Union.*

The next day American diplomats brought the situation before the United Nations and the Organization of American States using declassified photographs to counter Soviet claims that no offensive weapons were being installed in Cuba. Khrushchev responded to Kennedy's communication in a letter that, typical of his style, contained threats and appeals to reason:

> *The Soviet Government considers that the violation of the freedom to use international waters and international air space is an act of aggression which pushes mankind toward the abyss of a world nuclear-missile war.... Naturally we will not simply be bystanders with regard to piratical acts by American ships on the high seas. We will then be forced on our part to take the measures we consider necessary and adequate in order to protect our rights. We have everything necessary to do so.*

Actually, he didn't. The Soviet Union could threaten much of Western Europe and parts of the US, but such an attack would have been an act of national suicide. Khrushchev knew that America's nuclear stockpile was much larger, more reliable and would devastate the Soviet Union. Woodrow Wilson Center scholar Robert S. Norris estimated that:

> ...*a large scale attack by the United States against the Soviet Union in October 1962 would have been with over 3500 ("fully generated") nuclear weapons, with a combined yield of approximately 6300 megatons. This was about half of the number of warheads with US strategic forces....*

By contrast, he wrote that the Soviets had "approximately 42 ICBMs capable of reaching the United States, no SLBMs, and a long-range bomber force of 160 Bear and Bison bombers that would have had to face a formidable US–Canadian air defense system...."

On October 26, the US Navy stopped and searched a Soviet chartered cargo ship heading for Cuba. The Soviets did not interfere or provoke a faceoff on the high seas. Fidel Castro, who was unaware of the Soviet's comparatively weak military position, wrote to Khrushchev on the same day, seemingly urging a nuclear first strike against the US in response to an invasion:

> ...*I believe that the imperialists' aggressiveness makes them extremely dangerous, and that if they manage to carry out an invasion of Cuba—a brutal act in violation of universal and moral law—then that would be the moment to eliminate this danger forever, in an act of the most legitimate self-defense.*

However harsh and terrible the solution, there would be no other.

The next day a Soviet missile battery shot down an American surveillance aircraft overflying an area near the US base at Guantanamo Bay, killing the pilot, Major Rudolph Anderson. The US military recommended an immediate attack on SAM sites, but the President denied the request, believing that the shoot down had not been authorized by the Soviets. He was wrong. Washington Post reporter Michael Dobbs discovered many years later while researching Soviet archives for his book *One Minute to Midnight* that the shoot down was no accident. Generals Leonid Garbuz, deputy commander of Soviet forces in Cuba, and Stepan Grechko, commander of Soviet anti-aircraft forces, made the deliberate decision to shoot down Major Anderson's plane:

I expressed the view that all our missile starting positions had been uncovered, and we must not allow that the secret information to fall into the hands of the Pentagon. Stepan Naumovich several times tried to get in touch with our commander [General Issa Pliyev] but we did not succeed in finding him in the crucial minutes. It was also impossible to get in touch with Moscow in such a short time. We knew that Pliyev had more than once asked [Defense Minister] Malinovsky to allow him to shoot down American spy planes, but had received no answer. After a short period of reflection, S.N. Grechko announced, "Well, let's take responsibility ourselves."[45]

The President, acting on limited information, had once again misread the events. His lack of awareness would have been costly if he had authorized an invasion of the island expecting only a conventional response from the Cubans. American troops would have faced a much stronger enemy than anticipated, buttressed by thousands of Soviet troops armed with tactical nuclear weapons.

Khrushchev's Sleight of Hand

One of the riskiest points in a difficult negotiation occurs when a resolution seems very close. Experienced negotiators will often sneak a provision or line into the final agreement or choose more beneficial language hoping that the other side will just go along. That's exactly what the Soviets did. Khrushchev carefully gave Kennedy what he specifically asked for, not what he actually wanted. His letter of agreement to the President stated that Soviets troops had been directed to "**dismantle** *the arms you describe as offensive [emphasis added]*, and to crate and return them to the Soviet Union." It said nothing about the tactical nuclear weapons and cruise missiles unknown to the US, which Khrushchev was planning to secretly transfer to Cuban control.

Why would Khrushchev take such a risk? Castro was reportedly furious that the Soviets had backed down to American pressure. Khrushchev wanted to salvage the relationship, so he sent his most dependable troubleshooter, Prime Minister Anastas Mikoyan, to reassure Castro that the

Soviets had his back. Mikoyan recommended to the senior Soviet leadership before leaving for Cuba that Soviet tactical nuclear weapons already on the island be turned over to Castro's control. Soviet advisors would train the Cubans and then leave them to use the weapons as they saw fit.[46] The plan was approved as a tactic to reassure Castro and protect Cuba from future American invasion.

Mikoyan met with Castro in Havana and explained the situation: "You know that not only in these letters but today also, we hold to the position that you will keep all the weapons with the exception of the 'offensive' weapons and associated service personnel, which were promised to be withdrawn in Khrushchev's letter."[47] According to Soviet documents, it was Castro's unruly, unmanageable personality that ultimately convinced Mikoyan and the Soviet government that they should pull all nuclear weapons out of the island.

Khrushchev had been willing to transfer Soviet nuclear weapons to an important, but by no means crucial ally at the risk of another crisis and potential nuclear war with the United States.[48] His actions before and during the crisis demonstrated how otherwise rational leaders sometimes recklessly gamble with the lives of millions in the pursuit of questionable advantage.

Implications

These crises demonstrate that nuclear weapons do not reliably deter decision makers from engaging in brinksmanship and reckless decision making. Khrushchev repeatedly took chances and risked nuclear confrontations with the United States throughout his years as leader of the Soviet Union. This was a period characterized by American nuclear superiority, yet it did not deter Khrushchev from risking the future of his nation and millions of lives.

These events also demonstrate that preventing nuclear conflict requires an effective strategy and clear understanding of vital national interests. Eisenhower was able to leverage America's nuclear arsenal to deter adversaries and buttress diplomacy in the service of national security. His personal credibility, earned as America's leading general during World War II, magnified the impact of his policies. But credibility is not easily transferable to a new, unproven leader, as demonstrated by Khrushchev's willingness to bully Kennedy out of Berlin and his attempt to introduce nuclear missiles into Cuba.

For all of his blustering, Khrushchev was more careful with his brinksmanship when he faced Eisenhower than Kennedy. At no time did he intentionally and forcefully challenge Eisenhower as he did the younger American President in Vienna, Berlin and Cuba.

The strengths and weaknesses of intelligence were also in evidence during the Cuban Missile Crisis. The CIA acquired better information and more accurately assessed its implications during that crisis. Yet it, along with military intelligence agencies, overestimated Soviet strategic nuclear capabilities and underestimated Soviet tactical nuclear strength on the island. As a result, Kennedy made important decisions, such as selecting the blockade over airstrikes and invasion, with incomplete, inaccurate information. Interestingly, it was Khrushchev, the one decision maker with the most accurate, complete information, who bluffed and recklessly risked the destruction of his country over objectives of limited strategic value.

Finally, documents in Soviet archives, interviews with key participants and research by scholars (including Mikoyan's son), revealed that the Soviets were willing to proliferate nuclear weapons to their newfound Cuban client. This was no empty scheme and should give pause to those who think that other nuclear powers, most notably Iran, would never transfer tactical nuclear weapons to a valued ally like Hezbollah.

{ 4 }

Accidental Risks

One of the structural weaknesses in many experts' analysis of decision making and decision makers in a future nuclear Middle East is their almost exclusive focus on the intentional use of nuclear weapons. While national policies on nuclear weapons are important, some of the most dangerous incidents, crises and close calls of the Cold War were not caused by the planned use of nuclear weapons. They were caused when routine operations were disrupted and normal decision making was upset by unexpected failures in technology, processes and human performance. We were saved from the unimaginable horrors of nuclear war by verification procedures, courageous decision makers and, all too often, luck. It is a foregone conclusion that similar failures will occur in a future nuclear Middle East environment in which Iran and Israel will be keeping weary eyes on each other.

These are important considerations because technology is often promoted as a solution to improve stability and prevent accidental nuclear conflict. In this context, the superpowers can help both sides by supplying them with proven systems to prevent a surprise nuclear first strike. The United States has provided Israel with cutting-edge military technologies such as the Patriot air defense systems.[49] Russia has drawn closer to Iran in recent years, at least commercially, and following the recent nuclear agreement and lifting of UN sanctions decided to offer the Islamic Republic advanced S-300 Air Defense Systems.[50]

High tech systems helped the superpowers improve early detection of missile launches; but they were no panacea. The incidents in this chapter unintentionally moved the world closer to an unplanned, unwanted nuclear exchange than American and Soviet leaders had anticipated. Thankfully, most false warnings were identified and alerts deescalated by human intervention and verification processes developed and improved over many years. It's not clear, however, that these methods will prove equally effective in a nuclear Middle East. The incidents discussed below illustrate some of their limits and shortcomings, and their implications for a future nuclear standoff in the region.

The Armageddon Training Tape Incident

On November 9, 1979, a training tape was mistakenly loaded onto the North American early warning computer systems.

The software displayed a realistic scenario of a massive incoming Soviet nuclear first strike at the North American Defense Command's (NORAD) Cheyenne Mountain Complex in Colorado Springs, the Pentagon National Military Command Center in Washington, and the Alternate National Military Command Center in Fort Ritchie, Maryland. The imaginary nightmare scenario triggered alerts to Minuteman ICBM missile silos and the continental air defense system, which launched some of its fighters. Even the National Emergency Airborne Command Post (the "doomsday plane") was sent up, although the President was not aboard.

The event triggered attack warning verification processes that immediately convened a threat assessment team of senior officers from the three command centers. They were provided with independent early warning satellite and radar data, which showed no signs of a Soviet missile attack. The assessment team quickly concluded that it was a false warning and canceled the alert. The verification process, which had been developed, tested and improved with experience, allowed the assessment to be completed in a fraction of the time Soviet missiles would have taken to reach American land-based ICBMs.

To be practical, a warning verification process has to execute fast enough to allow the national command authority time to consider the situation and issue launch orders before enemy missiles reach their targets. In this particular case, American land-based ICBM firing preparation actually began while the independent assessment was taking place, which ensured missiles could be fired with minimum delay. Thankfully, that order never came, and the alert was canceled. The cause of the false alarm was identified in the investigation that followed.

Chip Malfunction at the Mountain

On June 3, 1980, less than a year after the training tape incident, the failure of a computer chip at NORAD's Cheyenne Mountain Complex triggered another incoming missile attack warning. In this case, the warning systems at the Mountain displayed erratic information showing different numbers of incoming missiles. Unlike the training tape incident, the other command centers were not affected, and it quickly became apparent that a technical glitch had triggered a false alarm. The same verification procedures used in the training tape incident convened a senior assessment team that evaluated independent warning information before canceling the alert.

The Man Who Saved Our World

September 26, 1983, was a dry, warm day in Denver, Colorado. The temperature hovered around 83°F just after three o'clock in the afternoon. Life went on as usual for millions of Coloradans as kids left school for the day to enjoy the warm weather. Unbeknownst to them, events were unfolding miles above the earth that would soon put their lives and millions of others in terrible peril.

On the other side of the world, it was just after midnight in Moscow, where Colonel Stanislav Petrov was settling down to another shift as the command officer of a secret early warning system bunker. It was designed to receive and process alerts from a new family of satellites looking for signs of a US missile launch against the Soviet Union.[51] These were difficult times for the Soviet leadership and people. The economy was stagnant, and the country was embroiled in a costly, difficult war in Afghanistan. Leonid Brezhnev, the long-serving leader of the Communist Party, had died the previous year, leaving former KGB chief Yuri Andropov in charge.

Andropov had been unsettled even before becoming First Secretary by secret studies and models indicating that the Soviet Union was falling behind the United States economically, technically and militarily. They essentially suggested that the Soviet Union had lost the Cold War. Now his country was facing a new US President, Ronald Reagan, who promised to further increase military spending and, most concerning to the Kremlin, had launched an initiative to deploy technically advanced systems to protect the US from missile attacks. These and other events had convinced many in the Soviet leadership that the US might be planning a nuclear first strike.[52]

Fears of American intentions had been conveyed to all military personnel, particularly those working in the early warning systems. Petrov was told on multiple occasions to be on alert because it looked as if the Americans were preparing to launch a preemptive attack against the Soviet Union. But all had been quiet as usual in the bunker that night, until shortly after midnight when the Colonel and his crew were startled by alarms and a flashing indicator that read "launch." The fate of millions would rest on his shoulders over the next five minutes as he considered the warnings and pondered his options. In an interview with the BBC thirty years after that fateful night, he described the series of events:

> *I had all the data [to suggest there was an ongoing missile attack]. If I had sent my report up the chain of command, nobody would have said a word against it... The siren howled, but I just sat there for a few seconds, staring at the big, back-lit, red screen with the word "launch" on it.... A minute later the siren went off again. The second missile was launched. Then the third, and the fourth, and the fifth. Computers changed their alerts from "launch" to "missile strike"....*[53]

Petrov took a few more minutes to consider the situation before deciding on his own that it was a false alarm. Why? After thinking through the logic of the warning, he concluded that "when people start a war, they don't start it with only five missiles.... You can do little damage with just five missiles."[54] He had to wait about twenty-two minutes before he could be completely sure that it was a false alarm. That's how long it would have taken US missiles to reach the Soviet Union. It had come down to a judgment call, with the fate of his country and the world in the balance. What caused the false alarm? The new Soviet early detection satellites were spoofed by the position of the sun, reflections off American missile fields and cloud cover. The system was new and may not have been tested under those particular conditions.[55]

Had Colonel Petrov sent the alert up the chain of command, the Soviet leadership would have had less than twenty minutes in the middle of the night, while fearful of American intentions and under high uncertainty, to decide if the warning was caused by an American preemptive attack requiring an immediate retaliatory response. We will never know what they would have decided, of course, but our odds of surviving September 26, 1983, were significantly improved by Petrov's good judgment and courageous decision making.

Why was he able to rely on his judgment instead of strictly following protocol? He credits his civilian education, which set him apart from others in the bunker that night: "My colleagues were all professional soldiers, they were taught to give and obey orders...they were lucky it was me on shift that night."

The Research Rocket Scare

Sometimes events unfold as expected and technology operates flawlessly, but then disaster strikes when unconnected activities cross paths, creating conditions unaccounted for by engineers and operators. This dynamic led to another close call on January 25, 1995, when a team of Norwegian and American weather scientists launched a large research rocket from Andoya Island, off the coast of Norway.[56] At 18.4 meters long with a weight of about six tons, the rocket was atypical in size, configuration and performance. It used the first stage of an old American tactical missile as one of three to boost the rocket and instruments to high altitude on a trajectory away from Russia. This is when the scientists' activities and the still unwinding Cold War crossed paths in ways they hadn't foreseen.

The trajectory of the weather rocket, which led away from Russia, followed the path that a Trident Missile fired from a US nuclear submarine would travel to detonate and blind Russian early warning and communication systems.[57] The Russians had considered this scenario as a prelude to an American preemptive attack and had coded it into their early warning systems. They also had a library of American rocket profiles that included the old American tactical missile stage used in the weather rocket.

The research rocket was picked up by Russian missile detection systems and classified by computers as a potential American nuclear missile launch, triggering a warning. There is some controversy over whether Russian President Boris Yeltsin's "football"—a portable control unit that could be used to authorize the launch of a retaliatory strike—actually sounded an alarm; if so, it would have been a first. He claimed that it had, but that independent satellite and radar information quickly showed that there was no incoming first strike. The event was classified Secret by the Russian military but was leaked and made public a few years later.

Implications

Nuclear weapons changed the landscape of war, diplomacy and foreign relations. Their destructive capacity caused the superpowers to develop and deploy increasingly sophisticated systems to detect missile launches and preemptive first strikes. The lesson was clear: If either superpower was caught unprepared by a nuclear first strike, then it would effectively cease to be a superpower within a few hours.

To put it in perspective, the Japanese attack on Pearl Harbor on December 7, 1941, was carried out by 353 airplanes in two waves; the first came at 7:53 AM and the second at 8:55 AM. The attacks lasted about two hours, killed 2,403 Americans, and destroyed or damaged 19 US Navy ships and 188 aircraft.[58,59] By contrast, a two-hour surprise attack with nuclear weapons could kill tens of millions, destroy a nation's ability to retaliate and turn dozens of metropolitan areas, government institutions and military command centers into smoldering ruins.

The Soviet Union and United States employ sophisticated technologies to detect enemy missiles as soon as they are launched. Radar nets spread around the globe can detect Intercontinental Ballistic Missiles (ICBMs) as they rise into the atmosphere; underwater detectors help track nuclear missile submarines; and satellites constantly monitor missile fields for early signs of unexpected launches. Distance is critical because it takes over half an hour for American and Russian missiles to reach their targets on the other side of the world. That golden half-hour provides valuable time to verify warnings and deescalate false alarms.

Computers have increased the sophistication and speed with which warning information is analyzed and verified. There are drawbacks, however, because these increasingly complex environments often introduce failure modes that were never accounted for by designers and operators. This is a characteristic of all complex systems and has caused numerous catastrophic failures in industries as diverse as finance and commercial flight operations.

Yale sociologist Charles Perrow investigated human behaviors, technical failures and incidents involving complex systems and coined the phrase "normal accident" to describe how many failures are actually normal, unintended system behaviors. They can occur, for example, when a disturbance triggers undesirable behaviors in a different part of the system, or in other interconnected systems. These synergistic effects are difficult to map, predict and understand beforehand. Unfortunately, they can unravel performance in ways that overwhelm operators by creating situations they were never trained to handle.

The most challenging normal accidents take place in systems that Perrow described as "tightly coupled," meaning that a failure in one part of a system will have prompt, significant impacts on one or more interconnected systems or subsystems. The key variable with tightly coupled systems is time, because unwanted behaviors (failures) happen so quickly that operators don't have time to diagnose problems and formulate a thoughtful response.

For example, the missile warning systems of the United States and Russia are integrated and technically complicated, but not "tightly coupled" because operators and decision makers have nearly 30 minutes to evaluate missile launch warnings and determine if they are valid. Unfortunately, the geography of the Middle East renders many proven American and Russian verification processes impractical. The relatively shorter distances between Iran and Israel reduce missile flight times from half an hour to between four and six minutes,[60] which renders independent verification and thoughtful assessment impractical. The four- to six-minute missile flight times effectively leave Iran and Israel with a tough choice: (1) wait and hope that a missile warning is false or (2) launch on warning to prevent an enemy first strike from destroying their land-based missiles and leaving them helpless. Cold War experiences suggest that a launch-on-warning policy will virtually guarantee a nuclear exchange.

Conclusions

I spent the first fifteen years of my career working in high-performance organizations operating dangerous technologies: six years on Air Force flight lines and eleven years supporting nuclear power plant operations (there was a two-year overlap). There is one central lesson I learned from my experiences and those of colleagues around the world: In operations, things can go wrong, sometimes very wrong. Accidents, mistakes, human and equipment failures happen, in spite of our best efforts and dedication to preventing them. Consequential decisions sometimes have to be made under stress and uncertainty—and sometimes a decision maker will make the wrong call.

When it comes to avoiding an unplanned, unwanted nuclear war, it is reckless to rely on tightly coupled systems with little margin for error in environments where the most logical option may be to launch on warning. The superpowers invested billions over many years to deploy technologies and develop verification methods specifically intended to prevent such gambles. Yet that may become the only practical operational model for Israel and Iran in a not-too-distant nuclear standoff.

{ 5 }

Existential threats

It helps to channel your inner Sherlock Holmes when researching decision making over half a century ago. History provides the backdrop and scores, which are valuable, but also subjects us to the damaging effects of creeping determinism. In hindsight, we tend to think that things turned out the way they were supposed to all along and forget the many places where a simple turn of events might have changed everything. By focusing on decision making and decision makers, we learn from choices made and those foregone, actions taken and those set aside. We can delve into the thinking of the individuals involved. It's an opportunity to learn from our predecessors' exercise of judgment under stress and uncertainty, which helps to put outcomes in greater context.

The downside of this approach is the hard, time-consuming work involved. Focusing on outcomes is relatively simple by comparison because we generally know what happened. Thankfully when it comes to the Cold War, the United States declassified and made available libraries of documents that include National Security Council discussions, State Department meetings and exchanges between key figures of the time. Likewise, after the collapse of the Soviet Union, Russia opened historic archives that contained information on iconic events such as the Cuban Missile Crisis. Many documents have been translated, organized and made available through online collections, such as *Foreign Relations of the United States*, hosted by the libraries of the University of Wisconsin-Madison and University of Illinois at Chicago. Others include detailed information about the Cuban Missile Crisis accessible through the National Security Archive at George Washington University's Gelman Library. These documents made it possible for researchers to better understand the thinking and judgments of decision makers whose choices decades ago determined the fate of millions.

As discussed in previous chapters, American President Dwight Eisenhower faced a growing existential threat to the United States in the early 1950s from an emerging nuclear power, the Soviet Union. He considered a variety of options, all of which included developing the capacity to destroy the Soviet Union as a functioning society. Soviet Premier Nikita Khrushchev understood the implications and responded in part by blustering and bluffing to hide his nation's comparatively weak position. He managed to worry key American allies, particularly Britain, into lobbying

Washington to avoid confronting the Soviets in places like Berlin—score one for Khrushchev! But the Soviet leader also convinced Eisenhower that the only solution to any significant American-Soviet conflict was total nuclear war. Khrushchev was fortunate that it never went that far, intentionally or accidentally.

Now there is an emerging nuclear standoff in the Middle East as Iran, in spite of the latest agreements, seeks to become a nuclear power, while a skeptical Israel is equally determined to prevent it. Israeli Prime Ministers and their Iranian counterparts will be following in American and Soviet footsteps, but their journey will be much different than the one traveled by the superpowers over half a century ago. Still, by judiciously applying Cold War lessons in decision making they may avoid some of the mistakes that on multiple occasions brought the superpowers closer to nuclear war than they wanted.

Defining Existential Threat

"Existential threat" is the latest in a long line of poorly defined terms that entered the Middle East's political lexicon. This lack of clarity is unfortunate because it is often cited as the likely driver of a preemptive attack by Israel and regional Sunni States on Iran. It is also rarely applied to Iran and what the Iranian leadership may consider similarly deadly threats against their nation.

Israeli Perspectives: Prime Minister Benjamin Netanyahu has consistently defined a nuclear-armed Iran as an existential threat to the State of Israel. He has not qualified his position with the number of nuclear weapons Iran must possess to reach existential threat status. Others, including Mossad Chief Tamir Prado, have been more nuanced than the Prime Minister. Prado reportedly remarked to a group of ambassadors in 2011:

> *What is the significance of the term existential threat? Does Iran pose a threat to Israel? Absolutely. But if one said a nuclear bomb in Iranian hands was an existential threat, that would mean that we would have to close up shop and go home. That's not the situation. The term existential threat is used too freely.*[61]

To most Israeli statesmen, even left-of-center former Prime Minister Shimon Peres, it is Iran's ability to produce nuclear weapons that would transform it into an existential threat to Israel, not the number of nuclear bombs in a future stockpile. As he framed it a year after Prado's remarks, "...humanity must learn the lessons of the Holocaust and stand up to existential threats before it is too late. Iran is at the center of this threat."[62] In practice, once a country has the demonstrated capacity to produce one nuclear weapon, then it could produce more of them. To most Israeli leaders, preventing Iran from gaining the capability to produce nuclear weapons is the critical objective.

The Ayatollahs' *View:* The concept of an existential threat in the Iranian context is more complex than in Israel's frame of reference. Existential threats, as portrayed by Supreme Leader Ayatollah Khamenei, generally revolve around the negative effects of Western secular influences on Islamic principles and Iranian culture. These threats are softer than those posed by nuclear weapons but, to the Ayatollahs atop Iran's power structure, no less destructive. Their views put in context the epithet Great Satan, first applied to the United States by the leader of the 1979 Iranian Revolution, Ayatollah Khomeini, and later by Khamenei, his successor. As noted Islamic scholar Bernard Lewis puts it, "Satan as depicted in the Qur'an is neither an imperialist nor an exploiter. He is a seducer, 'the insidious tempter who whispers in the hearts of men' (Qur'an CXIV, 4, 5)."[63] The current religious leaders of the Islamic Republic see the debilitating effects of western culture and secular materialism as existential threats to their nation.

Khamenei's singular determination to exclude external influences incompatible with his views of Islamic principles has led him to criticize and suppress internal dissent and traditional Iranian aspirations. It even led to a fallout with his protégé, former President Mahmoud Ahmadinejad, over the nationalist leanings of his government and the views of his top adviser Esfandiar Rahim Mashaei.

Mashaei had asserted that "… our understanding of the real nature of Iran and Islam is the Iranian school… Without Iran, Islam would be lost."[64] The nationalist tone of his position brought accusations of apostasy against him and the President from the religious leadership. These included a stern rebuke of Mashaei from the President's spiritual mentor, Ayatollah Mohammad Taghi Mesbah-Yazdi, who declared that "certain people who are shamelessly promoting the Iranian school in the place of the Islamic school are outsiders, not insiders... If somebody deviates from the right path, first we advise him and then we beat him with a stick."[65] The clear message was that nationalism at the expense of Islamism reeked of the West's secular materialism and would not be tolerated. To the Ayatollahs who sit at the top of the power pyramid in Iran, it is the Western secular and nationalistic influences that are the primary existential threats to *their* Islamic Republic.

Mutual Perspectives

Israel and Iran see each other through very different lenses. Israel has never viewed Iran as an illegitimate state and has no claims on its territory. Prior to the 1979 Islamic Revolution, the two countries enjoyed diplomatic relations, which Israel maintained even after the revolution. It was Ayatollah Khomeini who formally ended them by ejecting Israeli diplomats, closing down the Israeli Embassy and transferring the facilities to the Palestinian Liberation Organization. Israel later attempted to reestablish a less formal relationship with the new leadership and for a time both governments quietly took positive steps in that direction.

While Khomeini's anti-Israel rhetoric was severe, calling the US the Big Satan and Israel the Little Satan, actions spoke louder than words. The Israelis quietly helped the Iranians in their war with Iraq by channeling parts and providing technical support to keep the Iranian Air Force flying in spite of a US arms embargo.[66] It was an alliance of convenience for both countries, which would not last. The war ended in 1988 and Ayatollah Khomeini died a year later, leading to the ascendance of current Supreme Leader Khamenei.

As the Iran–Iraq war passed into history, Khamenei's rhetoric against Israel hardened, while calls for global Islamic Unity increased. There were two major barriers to that unity: Iran is Persian and Shi'a, while most of the region is Arab and Sunni. These communities have been adversaries for centuries and remain competitors for leadership in the Islamic world. There was one powerful issue, however, that could help bridge those differences, Palestine and what Sunni Arabs generally see as the Zionist occupation of traditionally Muslim lands.

Khamenei understood that the two most galvanizing desires in the Arab Middle East were the destruction of Israel and its replacement with a Palestinian State. He concluded that active Iranian leadership in opposing Israel would help bridge the differences between Shia and Sunni, Persians and Arabs, to Teheran's advantage. He also saw an opportunity to drive a wedge between the US and its Arab partners in the region by framing and opposing America as a "Zionist Puppet." The strategy advanced Iranian hegemony and leadership in the region at the expense of Saudi Arabia and other Sunni governments. Nationalism, which was criticized in the case of President Ahmadinejad, was apparently acceptable when cloaked in Khamenei's Shi'a Islamist ideology.

The drive to promote Iranian influence and hegemony in the region helps explain in part why the Supreme Leader appears obsessed with supporting the Palestinians, an issue that observers point out has little relevance to regular Iranians who are not burdened by Palestinian refugees, have long hosted the largest Jewish community in the Middle East outside of Israel and are not affected in their daily lives by Israel's existence, much less its foreign policy.[67] Israel is only a threat to Iran because Khamenei intentionally turned Iran into a threat to Israel—the Jewish State is an enemy of choice, not history.

Khamenei's Strategy to Eliminate Israel

Khamenei reiterated his strategy for eliminating the State of Israel in a recent tweet. His solution, framed as answers to nine questions, specifically excludes the massacring of Jews living in Israel, calling instead for those who immigrated to Israel to be "persuaded to leave." A referendum would then be held in which all original Palestinians, Christians and Jews, no matter where they live, could vote and select a government, which would decide whether remaining Jewish immigrants could stay or must return to their home countries.

The Supreme Leader acknowledged that "we do not expect the usurper Zionists to easily surrender to this proposal...." His solution to ultimately persuade them "is a resolute and armed confrontation." This includes arming and supporting Palestinians in the West Bank and providing continued support for Hezbollah's operations against the Israeli military in the North and Golan Heights. He does not recommend "...a classical war by the army of Muslim countries nor to throw migrated Jews at sea and certainly not an arbitration by UN or other international organizations."[68]

Khamenei expanded on these ideas in his book *Palestine*, which he recently published in Iran. According to Amir Taheri, who obtained a copy, the Supreme Leader is calling for a long period of warfare inside Israel "designed to make life unpleasant if not impossible for a majority of Israeli Jews so that they leave the country." He rejects any kind of two-state solution, insisting that Israel is a "cancerous tumor" that has no right to exist. He promotes tactics like those employed by Hezbollah units in Lebanon, which proved effective in previous confrontations with Israeli security forces. Khamenei points out that Iranians "have intervened in anti-Israeli matters, and it brought victory in the 33-day war by Hezbollah against Israel in 2006 and in the 22-day war between Hamas and Israel in the Gaza Strip."[69]

Khamenei recognizes in his writings that as long as Israel continues to garner international support, particularly from the United States, it can continue to exist. Part of his strategy is to make the increasingly violent conflict in Israel seem costly and intractable so that the international community will look for "a practical and logical mechanism" to resolve it.[70]

Where Nuclear Weapons Come In

Khamenei doesn't mention nuclear weapons in his strategy for destroying the State of Israel or when discussing the American presence in the Gulf. He, like Ayatollah Khomeini, has issued a legal ruling (fatwa) against the use of nuclear weapons. So, you might ask, why would Iran want to become a nuclear power? One reason is to deter Israel from retaliating or threatening to retaliate with nuclear weapons in response to Iranian promoted, organized and funded terrorism. The Israeli retaliation option would be effectively nullified by an Iranian nuclear capability. A nuclear Iran may cause Israel to think twice before taking aggressive actions against Hezbollah in Lebanon and Hamas in Gaza and the Palestinian Territories. This is an important consideration given the role of terrorism and violence in Khamenei's anti-Israel strategy.

Israel has raised concerns that Iran may provide allies like Hezbollah with tactical nuclear capabilities to deter Israeli attacks like the 1982 invasion of Lebanon. While some scholars scoff at this possibility, claiming that nuclear weapons are "too valuable" and Iran would not want to risk Israeli retaliation should Hezbollah use them,[71,72] there is a close Cold War precedent in Soviet plans to arm Cuba's military with tactical nukes in the aftermath of the Cuban Missile Crisis. In that case, it was Fidel Castro's inexperience and unreliability that led the Soviets to scrap their plans. Hezbollah's leadership is unlikely to raise similar concerns given its history as a close and reliable Iranian ally with a proven record fighting Israeli forces.

The Asymmetric Threat of a Nuclear Iran

Some experts see a future Israeli–Iranian nuclear standoff as akin to the Cold War between the US and Soviet Union. Academics such as the late Kenneth Waltz framed them as largely analogous and predicted similar outcomes if both Iran and Israel became nuclear powers, i.e. greater regional stability and coexistence. Setting aside the optimistic portrayal of a "stable Cold War," the two situations are actually fundamentally different due in large part to inherent threat asymmetries between Iran and Israel, which were absent in the American–Soviet standoff. Specifically, in an Iranian–Israeli Cold War, the Islamic Republic would enjoy overwhelming structural advantages that Israel could not counter through defensive technologies alone, not even with advanced American weapon systems.

Differences in geography, population and population distribution make Israel structurally much more vulnerable to nuclear attack than its adversary. Israel's land area is less than 1.5 percent that of Iran's, the world's seventeenth largest country (8,630 square miles vs. 636,374 square miles, respectively).[73,74] Iran's population is estimated at over ten times that of Israel (81.824 vs. 8.049 million);[75] the population of Teheran alone, 8.353 million, exceeds Israel's total. More importantly, much of the population that defines the modern State of Israel resides within a small geographic area comprising the districts of Tel-Aviv (71.81 square miles, population 1.339 million) and HaMerkaz (499 square miles, population 1.976 million), plus a relatively few large cities and metropolitan areas.

As a nation, Israel's highly concentrated population and critical infrastructure makes it an ideal target for tactical nuclear weapons, relative to a country with the size, population and geographic spread of Iran. The threat calculus between them is fundamentally different from the superpowers' during the Cold War. It's entirely reasonable for an Iranian arsenal of two dozen nuclear bombs (and the missiles to deliver them) to represent an existential threat to Israel, while an Israeli capability twice as large would not threaten Iran's national existence. These geographic, infrastructure and population differences, which cannot be practically undone, make a nuclear Middle East more one-sided and threatening to Israel than the Cold War was for either the United States or the Soviet Union.

Implications

Khamenei's stated strategy against Israel and his drive to turn the Iranian Republic into a nuclear power ignores lessons from the Cold War. There will be significant risks and high uncertainties for the Islamic Republic if it threatens Israel's existence and vital national interests before it joins the nuclear club. The United States and Soviet Union generally avoided actively threatening each other that way. The Cuban Missile Crisis is one exception where Soviet actions were seen as a direct provocation and threat to American national security, and it nearly led to a global nuclear war.

Israel has clear advantages at this point in technology and nuclear capabilities. It is estimated that the Jewish State has produced enough weapons-grade nuclear material to build 100 to 200 bombs, and that it keeps about 100 in its stockpile.[76] The challenge for the Israeli military is in delivering their nuclear arsenal to targets in Iran because, while the Israeli Air Force can reach its Arab neighbors, much of Iran remains outside the operational range of its aircraft. That leaves Medium and Intermediate Range Ballistic Missiles (M/IRBM), such as the Jericho-2 and the new Jericho-3, as the primary nuclear delivery systems.[77]

Iran does not have nuclear weapons at this time, and its MRBMs are not as technologically advanced and accurate as the Jericho-2/3s. It does have an ambitious and active missile research and development program expected to produce more advanced and accurate solid fuel missiles, such as the Sejjil, which has been in the testing phase for about eight years.[78] It is likely, therefore, that Iran will have an advanced MRBM by the time it moves to produce nuclear weapons in five to ten years, as many in the international community expect.[79]

A nuclear standoff between Israel and Iran will almost certainly depend on land-based nuclear-armed missiles. Israel has few options at this point and for the foreseeable future. Iran has the additional option of relying on proxies, namely Hezbollah and potentially Palestinian organizations like Hamas, to threaten Israel. That would put Hezbollah and Hamas in the crosshairs of the Israeli military, which frequently retaliates in the aftermath of attacks on its territory. Iranian proxies would need protection from Israeli retaliation if Iran expects them to increase external attacks and internal acts of terrorism against the Jewish State. Nuclear missiles would provide Iran with options to directly threaten Israel and deter Israeli attacks on its allies.

Another option for Iran to protect key allies like Hezbollah from the threat of an Israeli retaliatory ground offensive is to provide them with tactical nuclear weapons, as the Israeli government has warned. While some have scoffed at the idea, targeted proliferation to key allies is supported by Cold War precedent in Cuba.

The challenge for Iran going forward will be to become a nuclear power without triggering a preemptive Israeli attack. Cold War precedent supports the consideration of a preemptive strategy to prevent the development and deployment of enemy nuclear weapons. In the early 1950s, US President Eisenhower actively discussed a preemptive conflict to eliminate the Soviet Union as a nuclear threat. He wondered in a letter to Secretary of State Dulles if "we would be forced to consider whether or not our duty to future generations did not require us to initiate war at the most propitious moment that we could designate."[80] The challenge for Israel will be to prevent Iran from becoming a nuclear power, preferably without relying on a preemptive conflict to achieve it. But if no alternative becomes available, preemption may become preferable to an existentially threatening standoff.

Iran and Israel will face economic challenges developing, deploying and sustaining credible nuclear deterrents. In the early years of the nuclear age, US Presidents Truman and Eisenhower struggled to support strong nuclear and conventional forces. Truman was forced to ask for a tax hike, and Eisenhower worried about the effect of high taxes and defense spending on the economy. Ike's strategy reduced spending on conventional forces to offset higher spending on nuclear weapons. The downside of that strategy was a decrease in military flexibility and greater reliance on the threatened use of nuclear weapons.

This is an important consideration for Iran and particularly for Israel, which would need comparatively larger nuclear capabilities to deter Iran and a strong conventional military to deal with recurrent threats from its neighbors and terrorist groups. If Israel is forced by Iranian nuclear capabilities to tilt its security strategy towards nuclear deterrence, then it may have to rely on nuclear weapons in future conflicts with its neighbors because it will lack sufficient conventional forces.

This was the challenge in post-World War II Europe with Berlin and to a lesser degree West Germany because the West could not match the Soviets and later Warsaw Pact strength in armor, artillery and manpower. West European countries never invested enough in their conventional military to offset the East's strengths, even with American troops stationed on the continent. Most scenarios of a Soviet-Warsaw Pact push into Western Europe quickly escalated to NATO using tactical nuclear weapons.

Conclusion

A future nuclear standoff between Israel and Iran would be distinctly different than the superpowers' during the Cold War. There were instances early in the Cold War where the United State was in a dominant position (similar Israel's today) and wondered what to do as an emerging enemy threatened its existence. Eisenhower considered a preemptive nuclear war with the Soviet Union to eliminate that threat but ultimately decided against it for a variety of reasons.

Eisenhower also worried that the US had to protect its economy and social fabric from the effects of an arms race with the Soviets. He was concerned that national security needs could undermine economic performance and negatively influence American society by putting it on constant wartime alert. His solution was to deter communist expansionism and aggression through the threat of massive nuclear retaliation, paid for by reduced spending on conventional forces.

At the heart of Eisenhower's decision to tolerate a nuclear adversary was the recognition that the United States had a vastly superior economy and could deploy unmatched nuclear capabilities. Given Iran's much larger economy and the relatively modest nuclear capabilities it needs to effectively threaten Israel, Eisenhower's economic arguments don't hold in this case. This is not an abstract analysis. The Soviet Union collapsed in part because its economy could not support the levels of military spending required to match America's increases under Presidents Carter and Reagan.

If Iran deploys nuclear weapons in sufficient strength to neutralize Israel's current advantage, it will quickly enjoy superior strategic flexibility and advantage over Israel and the Sunni Arab States in the region. An Iranian nuclear capability would freeze Israel out of most of their options for retaliating against and deterring Iranian sponsored aggression.

The dilemma for Israel may come down to tolerating an Iranian existential threat, or preemptively destroying Iran's government and nuclear infrastructure. The dilemma for Iran is whether to risk a nuclear attack in the coming years by pursuing nuclear weapons and following through on its strategy to destroy its nuclear adversary. Lessons from the Cold War suggest that a preemptive nuclear war by Israel should not be discounted. While not an ideal choice, it may be the only one available to neutralize an emerging irreversible existential threat.

{ 6 }

Lessons Learned & Lost

The Cold War was arguably the most dangerous period in human history. Never before had governments possessed the power to destroy nations and kill millions in a matter of hours. In 1956, a select panel of scientists and scholars estimated that "a massive nuclear attack on the United States resulting in casualties of the order of 50,000,000 without drastically improved preparation of the people, would jeopardize support of the national government and of the war effort, and might well result in national disintegration."[81] This scenario would have been dismissed as alarmist science fiction before the bombings of Hiroshima and Nagasaki demonstrated the destructive power of the atom.

A general nuclear war at the height of the Cold War would have destroyed many, if not most, major population centers in the northern hemisphere, while contaminating surrounding areas for decades. The strain on world economies and social order would have delayed clean up and recovery efforts for years. And beyond the immediate death toll, the impact of radiation exposure on survivors is impossible to calculate. During the Cuban Missile Crisis, Joint Chiefs Chairman General Maxwell D. Taylor acknowledged that "there is no experience factor upon which to base an estimate of casualties" in the event nuclear weapons were used.[82] Thankfully, Cold War lessons were not written in blood; they were captured on paper and are now increasingly available online to those eager to learn from the past, so we can avoid catastrophes in the future.

As perilous as the Cold War actually was, the risks of an intentional or accidental nuclear exchange in a nuclear Middle East will be higher. The region is a worst-case operational environment for a nuclear feud, with conditions that promote launch-on-warning decisions that on multiple instances of the Cold War would have led to global nuclear war. This may not be intuitively clear from the historical–philosophical perspective common to policy making. But, when viewed from an operational, decision-making frame of reference, it becomes evident that a nuclear standoff in the Middle East will raise the risks of intentional, unintentional and accidental nuclear conflict beyond anything experienced by the superpowers. That is the most important and disconcerting lesson of the Cold War for Iran and Israel.

Cold, Hard Lessons

The end of the Cold War and collapse of the Soviet Union opened historical archives that revealed much of the thinking and decision making surrounding nuclear weapons and their role in Soviet and American national security strategy. For the first time, we can look behind critical events and consider the factors that influenced and constrained decision makers as they wrestled with the emerging threats, crises and uncertainties of nuclear conflict. In researching this book, I was able to review many of the documented assumptions, expectations, fears and judgments of decision makers on both sides and to compare their understanding of events at the time against outcomes we now take for granted.

The following is not a comprehensive list of Cold War lessons learned, but it helps illuminate some of the difficulties, risks and uncertainties inherent to a nuclear Middle East. Viewed together, they can help us visualize the technical and human challenges of nuclear deterrence and the implications of another risky standoff in a violent, unstable region of the world.

Lesson: Nuclear weapons have an abysmal record for deterring reckless risk-taking and conventional conflicts.

This counterintuitive conclusion surprised the Truman administration, which had planned to reduce conventional forces by relying on nuclear deterrence. The specter of nuclear weapons and war deeply concerned the democratic leaders of

Western Europe but did not deter communist leaders in the Soviet Union and Communist China from challenging the West in general or the United States in particular.

Stalin was not deterred by America's nuclear monopoly from installing communist governments across Central and Eastern Europe after WWII or from risking a showdown over Berlin in 1948–49. He and communist Chinese leader Mao Zedong encouraged and supported the 1950 invasion of South Korea by the communist North, and both sent equipment and soldiers to fight the US and its allies. During the 1950s and early '60s, Khrushchev triggered repeated crises over Berlin and risked global nuclear war by introducing medium-range nuclear missiles into Cuba.

Israel's nuclear arsenal has not protected it from attack by its neighbors and terrorist groups like Hezbollah. Nor has it deterred Iran, which has boasted of actively supporting and sponsoring terrorism against the Jewish State.

Lesson: The high costs of developing, producing and fielding nuclear weapons are not offset by savings in conventional defense costs.

The US spent nearly $25 billion in today's dollars on the Manhattan Project to produce its first three nuclear bombs. It has spent over a trillion dollars since then on its nuclear arsenal and delivery systems, even though US Presidents consistently decided not to use them in conflicts from Korea to Vietnam. International consensus and public opinion made nuclear weapons impractical substitutes for conventional munitions. The superpowers were thus forced to deploy both nuclear and conventional forces, which increased overall defense spending.

The expense of going nuclear can force greater reliance on nuclear weapons if conventional capabilities have to be sacrificed, as happened in the United States during the 1950s. A nuclear arms race in the Middle East is likely to increase defense costs, particularly in Israel, which will need a large nuclear arsenal on alert to effectively deter Iran. Iran's aggressive pursuit of military capabilities has already influenced defense spending in the region, as reflected in Israeli and Saudi defense budgets, the world's largest as a percentage of GDP.[83]

Lesson: Nations in a nuclear standoff must keep large numbers of nuclear weapons on constant alert.

Conventional wars allow countries to mobilize their military forces, economy and society over a period of time. A nuclear war, by contrast, would end in a matter of hours, not weeks, months or years. What matters in a nuclear conflict are the forces that can be launched against the enemy without delay, i.e. before those forces can be destroyed by incoming nuclear missiles.

Israel will need to change its policy of neither confirming nor denying that it has nuclear weapons. Once adversaries go nuclear, they need to make their deterrence explicit and unambiguous, as the Soviets and Americans did.[84]

Lesson: Nuclear weapons change the dynamics of a nation's internal power structure. They promote divergent, competing centers of power within the military and civilian sectors of the government.

Organizations involved with nuclear weapons gain in prestige and influence, while those with the power and authority to use them gain in relative power. The US government initially treated nuclear weapons as just another class of munitions and developed policies for their use. Truman quickly changed the process and retained all decisions for deployment and use in the White House. Eisenhower did the same, often frustrating the military services, which vied for their own, independent nuclear capabilities.

Truman worried about some commander in the military deciding to use nuclear weapons without his permission, so he kept the nuclear cores separate from the bomb casings, and under civilian control. The Soviets were not as clear establishing operational controls of their tactical nuclear weapons in Cuba, which left local commanders with the option of using them against American forces without direct Kremlin approval. It meant that a Soviet commander on a distant foreign island could have started World War III.

The Israelis and Iranians will have to contend with these issues if Iran goes nuclear. Unlike Truman and Eisenhower, they will have to keep much of their arsenal on alert and ready to launch. And with only minutes to decide whether to launch or risk losing their missiles, the most critical question will be who will have the authority to "push the button."

Lesson: Nuclear exchanges are more likely to occur by accident or through technical failure than by intention.

With few exceptions, most nuclear close calls during the Cold War were unplanned and unintended. Poor communications and an aggressive local commander in the 1961 Berlin Crisis, a training incident in an American early warning computer system, component failures at NORAD and spoofed Soviet satellites brought the world uncomfortably close to a nuclear exchange. There were many others, some still classified.

Unlike the Soviets and Americans, the Israelis and Iranians will have very little time to verify alarms and deescalate alerts. This is a major risk factor because it is likely that, in the absence of verification processes and formal procedures, there would have been one or more nuclear exchanges between the superpowers during the Cold War. Those strongly suggest that launch-on-warning protocols are unacceptably dangerous; yet that may be the most practical operational option in an Iranian-Israeli standoff.

Lesson: Nuclear weapons are sometimes shared with friends and allies.

During the Cold War, the United States shared nuclear weapons technology with its closest ally, Great Britain, while the Soviet Union helped Communist China set up its nuclear weapons development program, in spite of recurring tensions between them. The Soviet Union actively pursued a plan to transfer tactical nuclear weapons to Fidel Castro's government in 1962. There are multiple precedents for the transfer of nuclear weapons and related technologies based on shared commercial, national and ideological interests.

Lesson: Perceived or real, an existential threat increases the risk of a preemptive "defense."

The superpowers competed with each other during the Cold War in a variety of ways: through proxies, economic assistance, intelligence and conflicts in areas outside their territories. They interfered with each other's vital allies and attempted to woo them over, but in general they avoided intentional head-to-head confrontations that could escalate into nuclear war. There was tacit agreement to avoid creating intentional, direct, existential threats against each other. The one exception was Khrushchev's attempt to introduce medium range nuclear missiles into Cuba, which almost got out of his control.

Khamenei's strategy to destroy Israel has no direct parallel in the Cold War relationship between the superpowers. It is, by definition, intended as an existential threat, albeit without direct reliance on nuclear weapons or nuclear war. There is precedent in the Cold War for a nuclear power facing an emerging existential threat to seriously consider a preemptive attack to eliminate that threat. If Khamenei follows through with his stated terror-based strategy against Israel and his government continues to pursue nuclear weapons, then an Israeli preemptive attack, with the probable acquiescence of regional Sunni Arab governments, will become increasingly likely.

Implications

The Middle East is a fundamentally different theater for a nuclear standoff than the Soviet–American situation was after World War II. Cold War lessons offer little reassurance that an Israeli–Iranian nuclear standoff will be peacefully resolved. On the contrary, Soviet and American archives released over the past twenty years show that the Cold War was not a period in which enlightened leaders were uniformly thoughtful and careful to avoid nuclear confrontation. They sometimes miscalculated, misunderstood their opponents and sought advantage in risky schemes that more than once brought the world to the brink of a nuclear war neither side wanted. Technical systems and processes designed to detect and report potential first strikes, while indispensable for avoiding accidental nuclear conflict, failed in multiple instances and triggered the start of retaliation protocols. Time and technology gave the superpowers the option of independently verifying unexpected threats; in the Middle East, time is so limited that many Cold War verification protocols will be impractical.

The bottom line? Cold War lessons suggest that a nuclear standoff in the Middle East will be marked by much higher risks and uncertainties than faced by the superpowers in their four-decades-long adversarial relationship. They also suggest that given Iran's structural advantages, the possibility of an Israeli preemptive attack cannot be discounted.

{ 7 }

In Summary

When I began working on this book, I wondered if Israeli fears of a nuclear Iran were being magnified out of proportion by Israel's history of recurring wars and haunting memories of the Holocaust. I also wondered how the United States had dealt with similar nuclear threats when the Soviet Union became a nuclear power in the 1950s. American Presidents Truman and Eisenhower had stood by as a former ally turned into an increasingly threatening nuclear adversary, without resorting to preemptive war—why?

I ultimately concluded that both Presidents chose coexistence with the Soviets because they believed that, if war could be averted, the communist social and economic systems would ultimately fail. In the meantime, Soviet expansionism could be contained and aggression deterred by America's nuclear superiority and stronger economy. These were not easy choices and were not made by default; in practice, the specter of global nuclear war remained a real possibility throughout the Cold War.

The Israelis, by contrast, face a very different situation due to three specific factors: The Iranian government's declaration that Israel is not a legitimate nation and its explicit commitment to destroy the Jewish State; Israel's structurally weak position from which to face a nuclear Iran and survive even a limited nuclear exchange; and the Middle East's operational environment, which increases the risks of accidental nuclear war. Taken together, these factors technically support Israeli claims that a nuclear Iran will threaten its existence.

There are additional aggravating factors to consider based on Cold War experience and the Iranian Supreme Leader's strategy for destroying Israel. Khamenei's plot to sponsor increasing violence within Israel leaves the Jewish State with few options beyond aggressively responding against regional Iranian proxies, Hezbollah in particular. The ultimate check on Iranian conduct has been and remains Israel's undeclared nuclear capabilities. That check will disappear if Iran becomes a nuclear power. Even Israel's vaunted conventional superiority over Hezbollah could be rendered useless if Iran proliferates tactical nuclear weapons, as the Soviets had planned for Cuba in 1962.

The point is not to forecast Iran's future conduct or to predict a Middle East nuclear conflict. The point is that once Iran becomes a nuclear power, it will hold most, if not all, of the power advantages over Israel. And unless both nations reach a verifiable agreement never to put their nuclear forces on alert, an accidental nuclear war will be more than possible; Cold War experience suggests it will be likely. It took the superpowers decades to craft such agreements, even under conditions that made negotiations easier, i.e. they had ongoing diplomatic relations and were used to negotiating with each other. Those conditions don't exist between Israel and Iran and won't as long as Khamenei's view of Israel continues to guide Iran's foreign policy.

What Would Ike Have Done?

Did the United States face a threat from the Soviet Union in the 1950s comparable to what Israel would face from a nuclear Iran? Not in practice, although Khrushchev convinced Eisenhower that the Soviets had much greater nuclear capabilities than they actually possessed. Khrushchev was no Ayatollah bent on provoking a conflict with the US. He was rash, blusterous and had a penchant for brinksmanship, but when the US pushed back, he generally accepted compromise. The real risks were in the potential for a miscalculation or for an incident to suddenly get out of control, as nearly happened in Berlin and Cuba.

How would President Eisenhower have responded if his administration had faced an impending existential threat from a declared enemy with an active strategy to destroy the US? He was consistently clear that he would unleash a full nuclear attack on the Soviet Union if the Soviets threatened or attacked the United States, an American ally or another vital interest. He repeatedly rejected calls by members of the NSC, including his Secretary of State, for a more flexible response strategy, insisting that there was no such thing as a slowly escalating nuclear conflict. He made it explicit that the response to a military conflict with the Soviets would be total war, as he clarified during the 394th National Security Council (NSC) meeting on January 22, 1959:

War is after all waged for a purpose. Our purpose is to defend ourselves. To defend ourselves means that we must destroy the present threat to ourselves. Once we become involved in a nuclear exchange with the Soviet Union, we could not stop until we had finished off the enemy; that is, forced him to stop fighting. If at any point in the hostilities we agree to make terms with the enemy, we would only make terms which allayed the Communist threat to us....[85]

These were not philosophical musings. The NSC also discussed post-nuclear war policies to deal with "terms of enemy surrender, border and territorial arrangements, administration of enemy territory, and independence for national minorities...." Later, the President asked what objectives the US should have in a nuclear war with the Soviets, beyond hitting them hard. Joint Chiefs Chairman General Twining "responded by stating that we planned in the event of such a war 'to shoot the works' and not to apply our military power degree by degree against the enemy." During further discussions:

> *The President commented that the only form in which you could expect to get a peace offering would be from that side in the conflict which was putting up the white flag. The US will never do this so we should go ahead and hit the Russians as hard as possible. We could not do anything else. They, the Russians, will have started the war, we will finish it. That is all the policy the President said he had.*

Those who find comfort in the outcome of the Cold War and see parallels with a future Israeli–Iranian nuclear standoff fail to recognize Eisenhower's determination to destroy existential threats to the nation, with nuclear weapons if necessary. He was clear that an existential threat against the United States would not be tolerated. And if nuclear war came, he would make sure that the enemy would not be left with either the will or the means to threaten America again for generations.

Eisenhower's strategy will not necessarily become Israel's strategy, but it was conceived under conditions similar to those emerging in the Middle East. If Iran becomes a nuclear power, Israel's security position will be much more tenuous that anything the United States ever faced during the Cold War, which lends impetus to preemption as a necessary strategy to prevent that from happening.

Conclusion

The multi-year negotiations recently concluded between Iran and the P5+1 were a missed opportunity to remove the threat of nuclear war in the Middle East. The nuclear and economic superpowers representing the UN Security Council had the opportunity to assert that further nuclear proliferation would not be tolerated and that they were prepared to act in unison to prevent it. It would have made full compliance with the NPT non-negotiable and laid the foundation for the future elimination of most nuclear weapons. It would also have eliminated a future Iranian–Israeli nuclear standoff, the potential of a preemptive war and the possibility of an accidental nuclear conflict.

We have, instead, an evolving situation in which Iran is likely to continue pursuing nuclear weapons and the means to deliver them to Israel and beyond. And Israel will continue watching and weighing the costs of preemptively acting to keep Iran from going nuclear. While no one can forecast a final resolution, Cold War history suggests that a military clash between Israel and Iran is becoming increasingly likely.

The lessons of the Cold War are clear in their implications: The only certain way to prevent a nuclear war is to prevent adversaries from possessing nuclear weapons in the first place. Those who see greater peace and stability in a nuclear Middle East have misconstrued the lessons of history. Declassified Cold War records offer mounting evidence that the peaceful end of the Cold War was anything but predetermined. Those four decades were more a gamble than a stable stalemate.

How big was the gamble? Daniel Ellsberg quotes a study prepared in the 1960s for the military Joint Chiefs that projected 600 million casualties in the Soviet Union and China in the aftermath of a full American nuclear attack.[86] Add to those estimates two to three hundred million more deaths in Europe and North America, and totals quickly approach a billion lost lives. Most of us go through life without thinking about how lucky we are that the Cold War never became hot. Perhaps the international community has also largely forgotten—or maybe they never learned these lessons. That would go a long way to explain why so many seem complacent, if not complicit, in once again rolling the nuclear dice, this time in a worst-case environment within a violent, unstable region of the world.

About the Author

Ozzie Paez is a researcher, author, engineer and information systems expert whose services focus on helping leaders and decision makers make timely, informed decisions. He is the author of *Going Nuclear: The Influence of History and Hindsight on the Iranian Nuclear Negotiations* and the upcoming book, *Informed Decision Makers—And Other Myths and Fallacies*. He has spent over 20 years developing information systems, databases and software for business, government and military applications. In the aftermath of 9/11, he brought this experience to the study of decision making within radical movements and terrorist groups. His research into the background of radical Islamist groups, their culture, leadership and belief systems led to new insights into the factors and tactics used in recruiting new members and in fostering terrorism at home.

Mr. Paez has co-authored a variety of papers on topics such as military assistance to local authorities after 9/11; culture and security in the context of the April 2007 Virginia Tech shootings; and technical subjects related to information systems and software development. He has published dozens of posts about various aspects of decision making on his blog, ozziepaezdecisions.com, and in newsletters. His interest in history and foreign policy is fueled by his memories of growing up in Communist Cuba, where he learned at a young age that even repressive governments, unencumbered by legal or constitutional limits, are often blind to the implications of important events and emerging threats to their power. Mr. Paez is an American citizen and military veteran of the US Air Force.

LinkedIn: http://www.linkedin.com/in/ozziepaezlinkedin
Author's Website & Blog: http://ozziepaezresearch.com/
Decision-Making Blog: http://ozziepaezdecisions.com

References

[1] Kenneth N. Waltz, "Why Iran Should Get the Bomb," *Foreign Policy*, July/August 2012, https://www.foreignaffairs.com/articles/iran/2012-06-15/why-iran-should-get-bomb.

[2] Waltz, "Why Iran Should Get the Bomb."

[3] John Keegan, "Necessary or Not, Dresden Remains a Topic of Anguish," *The Telegraph*, October 31, 2005, http://www.telegraph.co.uk/comment/personal-view/3620700/Necessary-or-not-Dresden-remains-a-topic-of-anguish.html.

[4] "Bombing of Dresden," History, retrieved 5/21/2015, http://www.history.com/topics/world-war-ii/battle-of-dresden.

[5] "How Many People Died as a Result of the Atomic Bombings?," FAQ, Radiation Effects Research Foundation, retrieved 5/21/2015, http://www.rerf.or.jp/general/qa_e/qa1.html.

[6] Campbell Craig, *Destroying the Village: Eisenhower and Thermonuclear War* (Columbia University Press, 1998),149–150.

[7] Richard W. Stewart, General Editor, *American Military History, Volume II, The United States Army in a Global Era, 1917-2003* (United States Army, 2005), 201, http://www.history.army.mil/books/amh-v2/amh%20v2/chapter7.htm.

[8] Stewart, *American Military History,* 200.

[9] George T. Hodermarsky, "Postwar Naval Force Reductions 1945-1950: Impact on the Next War," United States Naval War College, 1990, 45, http://www.dtic.mil/dtic/tr/fulltext/u2/a227251.pdf.

[10] US Navy Personnel in World War II, Service and Casualty Statistics, Naval History and Heritage Command, US Navy, http://www.history.navy.mil/research/library/online-reading-room/title-list-alphabetically/u/us-navy-personnel-in-world-war-ii-service-and-casualty-statistics.html.

[11] Stewart, *American Military History,* 201.

[12] Telegram, George Kennan to George Marshall ["Long Telegram"], February 22, 1946. Harry S. Truman Administration File, Elsey Papers. Truman Library, https://www.trumanlibrary.org/whistlestop/study_collections/coldwar/documents/pdf/6-6.pdf.

[13] George Kennan, "The Sources of Soviet Conduct," *Foreign Affairs*, July 1947, https://www.foreignaffairs.com/articles/russian-

federation/1947-07-01/sources-soviet-conduct.

[14] "The Truman Doctrine, 1947," Milestones: 1945-1952, US Department of State, Office of the Historian, https://history.state.gov/milestones/1945-1952/truman-doctrine.

[15] David Blair, "The Mystery of Jan Masaryk's Cold War 'Suicide' Deepens," *The Telegraph*, January 7, 2004, http://www.telegraph.co.uk/news/worldnews/europe/czechrepublic/1451107/Mystery-of-Jan-Masaryks-Cold-War-suicide-deepens.html.

[16] "NSC-68, 1950," Milestones: 1945–1952, US Department of State, Office of the Historian, https://history.state.gov/milestones/1945-1952/NSC68.

[17] Harry Truman, "Statement by the President Reviewing Two Years of Experience with the Atomic Energy Act," July 24, 1948, Harry S. Truman Library and Museum, http://trumanlibrary.org/publicpapers/index.php?pid=1709&st=&st1=.

[18] Robert J. Donovan, *Conflict and Crisis: The Presidency of Harry S. Truman, 1945–1948* (University of Missouri Press, 1996), 410.

[19] Richard J. Samuel, Editor, *Encyclopedia of United States National Security* (Sage Publications, Inc., 2005), 786.

[20] John Foster Dulles, "A Policy of Boldness," *Life*, May 19, 1952.

[21] Mark G. Toulouse, *The transformation of John Foster Dulles* (Mercer University Press, 1986), 110.

[22] "Report to the National Security Council by the Executive Secretary on Restatement of Basic National Security Policy," June 10, 1953, NSC 153/1, US Department of State, Office of the Historian, https://history.state.gov/historicaldocuments/frus1952-54v02p1/d73

[23] Report to the National Security Council.

[24] "Khrushchev and the Twentieth Congress of the Communist Party," Milestones: 1953–1960, US Department of State, Office of the Historian, https://history.state.gov/milestones/1953-1960/khrushchev-20th-congress.

[25] Richard Cavendish, "Lavrenti Beria Executed," History Today, December 12, 2003, http://www.historytoday.com/richard-cavendish/lavrenti-beria-executed.

[26] Lindsey Parrott, "Truce is Signed Ending the Fighting in Korea," *New York Times*, July 27, 1953, http://www.nytimes.com/learning/general/onthisday/big/0727.html.

[27] Parrott, "Truce is Signed."

[28] Parrott, "Truce is Signed."

[29] Stephen Daggett, "Costs of Major US Wars," Congressional Research Service, July 24, 2008, http://fpc.state.gov/documents/organization/108054.pdf

[30] "Memorandum From the Assistant Secretary of State for Policy Planning (Smith) to Secretary of State Dulles," November 17, 1958, Foreign Relations of the United States 1958–1960, Volume XIX, China, Document 238, US Department of State, Office of the Historian, https://history.state.gov/historicaldocuments/frus1958-60v19/d238.

[31] Craig, *Destroying the Village*, 83–84.

[32] National Security Council Report, "Statement of Policy on US Policy on Berlin," December 13, 1957, Foreign Relations of the United States, 1955–1957, Volume XXVI, Central And Southeastern Europe, Document 213, US Department of State, Office of the Historian, https://history.state.gov/historicaldocuments/frus1955-57v26/d213.

[33] United States Department of State Office of Public Communication, "The Department of State Bulletin, Volume XL: 1019–1044," US Department of State, 1939, 88.

[34] Neil Carmichael, "A Brief History of the Berlin Crisis of 1961," National Records and Archives Administration, 3,http://www.archives.gov/research/foreign-policy/cold-war/1961-berlin-crisis/overview/berlin-wall-overview.pdf.

[35] John F. Kennedy, "The Berlin Crisis Speech," July 25, 1961, Historic Speeches, Presidential Rhetoric, http://www.presidentialrhetoric.com/historicspeeches/kennedy/berlincrisis.html.

[36] Peter Karsten, editor, *Encyclopedia of War and American Society*, Volumes 1–3, (Sage Publications, 2005), 74.

[37] Carmichael, "A Brief History," 5.

[38] Craig, *Destroying the Village*, 149–150.

[39] The following discussion is based on information available from the Kennedy Presidential Library and Museum, specifically "The World on the Brink: John F Kennedy and the Cuban Missile Crisis, 13 Days in October 1962," http://microsites.jfklibrary.org/cmc/.

[40] Timothy J. Botti, *Ace in the Hole* (Greenwood Press, 1996), 185–188.

[41] Glenn Fowler, "John A. McCone, Head of CIA in Cuban Missile Crisis, Dies at 89," *New York Times*, February 16, 1999, http://www.nytimes.com/1991/02/16/obituaries/john-a-mccone-head-of-cia-in-cuban-missile-crisis-dies-at-89.html.

[42] Botti, *Ace*, 187.

[43] Conversations with my father.

[44] Svetlana Savranskaya and Thomas Blanton, editors, with Anna Melyakova, "Last Nuclear Weapons Left Cuba in December 1962," National Security Archive Electronic Briefing Book No. 449, December 11, 2013, http://nsarchive.gwu.edu/NSAEBB/NSAEBB449/.

[45] Michael Dobbs, web posts related to his book, *One Minute to Midnight: Kennedy, Khrushchev and Castro on the Brink of Nuclear War* (Knopf, 2008), http://nsarchive.gwu.edu/nsa/cuba_mis_cri/dobbs/anderson.htm and http://nsarchive.gwu.edu/nsa/cuba_mis_cri/dobbs/gitmo.htm.

[46] "Telegram from A. I. Mikoyan to the CC CPSU, and Gromyko's Response," November 8 and 9, 1962, National Security Archives, George Washington University, http://nsarchive.gwu.edu/NSAEBB/NSAEBB449/docs/Doc%2013%201962.11.08-09%20Telegram%20from%20Mikoyan%20to%20the%20CC%20CPSU%20and%20Gromyko's%20Response.pdf

[47] Sergo Mikoyan (author) and Svetlana Savranskaya (editor), *The Soviet Cuban Missile Crisis: Castro, Mikoyan, Kennedy, Khrushchev and the Missiles of November* (Stanford University Press, 2012), 344.

[48] Svetlana Savranskaya, "Cuba Almost Became a Nuclear Power in 1962: The Scariest Moment in History Was Even Scarier Than We Thought," *Foreign Policy*, October 10, 2012, http://foreignpolicy.com/2012/10/10/cuba-almost-became-a-nuclear-power-in-1962/.

[49] Taylor Dinerman, "How Israel Learned To Love Missile Defense," *National Review*, July 17, 2014, http://www.nationalreview.com/article/382931/how-israel-learned-love-missile-defense-taylor-dinerman.

[50] Neil MacFarquhar, "Putin Lifts Ban on Russian Missile Sales to Iran," *New York Times*, April 13, 2015, http://www.nytimes.com/2015/04/14/world/europe/putin-lifts-ban-on-russian-missile-sales-to-iran.html?_r=0.

[51] Geoffrey Forden, "Reducing a Common Danger: Improving Russia's Early-Warning System," Cato Institute Policy Analysis, May 3, 2001, http://object.cato.org/sites/cato.org/files/pubs/pdf/pa399.pdf.

[52] Benjamin B. Fischer, "A Cold Ware Conundrum: The 1983

Soviet Ware Scare," Center for the Study of Intelligence, Central Intelligence Agency, July 7, 2008, https://www.cia.gov/library/center-for-the-study-of-intelligence/csi-publications/books-and-monographs/a-cold-war-conundrum/source.htm.

[53] Pavel Aksenov, "Stanislav Petrov: The Man Who May Have Saved the World," *BBC*, September 26, 2013, http://www.bbc.com/news/world-europe-24280831.

[54] "Common Danger," Forden, p. 5.

[55] "Common Danger," Forden, p. 6.

[56] "Common Danger," Forden, p. 6.

[57] Nikolai Sokov, "Could Norway Trigger a Nuclear War? Notes on the Russian Command and Control System," PONARS Policy Memo 24, Center for Nonproliferation Studies, Monterey Institute, October 1997, http://csis.org/files/media/csis/pubs/pm_0024.pdf.

[58] "Remembering Pearl Harbor," National World War II Museum, http://www.nationalww2museum.org/assets/pdfs/pearl-harbor-fact-sheet-1.pdf.

[59] "Attack at Pearl Harbor, 1941," Eyewitness to History, http://www.eyewitnesstohistory.com/pearl.htm (1997).

[60] Mustafa Kibaroğlu and Ayşegül Kibaroğlu, *Global Security Watch—Turkey: A Reference Handbook* (Greenwood Publishing Group, 2009), 129.

[61] Anthony H. Cordesman and Bryan Gold, *The Gulf Military Balance: The Missile and Nuclear Dimensions* (Center for Strategic and International Studies, 2014), 156.

[62] Raphael Ahren, "Would a Nuclear Iran Truly Pose an Existential Threat?," *Times of Israel*, February 21, 2015, http://www.timesofisrael.com/would-a-nuclear-iran-truly-pose-an-existential-threat-to-israel/.

[63] Bernard Lewis, *The Crisis of Islam* (Random House Trade Paperback Edition, 2004), 81.

[64] Yvette Hovsepian-Bearce, *The Political Ideology of Ayatollah Khamenei: Out of the Mouth of the Supreme Leader of Iran* (Routledge, 2015), 233.

[65] Hovsepian-Bearce, *The Political Ideology*, 233.

[66] Trita Parsi, *Treacherous Alliance: The Secret Dealings of Israel, Iran and the United States* (Yale University, 2007).

[67] Karim Sadjadpour, *Reading Khamenei: The Worldview of Iran's Most Powerful Leader* (Carnegie Endowment for International Peace, 2009), 19,

http://carnegieendowment.org/files/sadjadpour_iran_final2.pdf.
[68] Ayatollah Khamenei, "Why should and how can #Israel be eliminated? Ayatollah Khamenei's answer to 9 key questions," November 9, 2014, Twitter, https://twitter.com/khamenei_ir/status/531366667377717248.
[69] Amir Taheri, "Iran Publishes New Book on How to Outwit US and Destroy Israel," *New York Post*, April 1, 2015, http://nypost.com/2015/08/01/iran-publishes-book-on-how-to-outwit-us-and-destroy-israel/.
[70] Taheri, "Iran Publishes New Book."
[71] Ehsaneh I Sadr, "The Impact of Iran's Nuclearization on Israel," in *Military Power and International Politics*, Robert J. Art and Kenneth N. Waltz, editors, (Rowman & Littlefield Publishers, Inc., 2009), 376.
[72] Johnathan Tepperman, "Nuclear Weapons Can Keep You Safe," *Newsweek*, August 28, 2009, http://www.newsweek.com/how-nuclear-weapons-can-keep-you-safe-78907.
[73] "About Israel," Israeli Ministry of Foreign Affairs, http://www.mfa.gov.il/mfa/aboutisrael/land/pages/the%20land-%20geography%20and%20climate.aspx.
[74] Susanna Darwin, "How Big is Iran?," *Encyclopaedia Britannica*, February 2, 2007, http://blogs.britannica.com/2007/02/just-how-big-is-iran/.
[75] *The World Factbook*, Central Intelligence Agency, https://www.cia.gov/library/publications/the-world-factbook/index.html.
[76] Israel, Nuclear Weapons, Federation of American Scientists, January 8, 2007, http://fas.org/nuke/guide/israel/nuke/.
[77] Alon Ben-David, "Israel Tests Enhanced Ballistic Missile," *Aviation Week*, July 29, 2013, http://aviationweek.com/awin/israel-tests-enhanced-ballistic-missile.`
[78] Iran, "Missile," NTI, October 2015. Accessed September 9, 2015, http://www.nti.org/country-profiles/iran/delivery-systems/.
[79] David E. Sanger, "Suppose We Just Let Iran Have the Bomb," *New York Times*, March 19, 2006, http://www.nytimes.com/2006/03/19/weekinreview/19sanger.ART0.html?pagewanted=all&_r=0.
[80] Henry D. Sokolski, *Best of Intentions: America's Campaign Against Strategic Weapons Proliferation* (Praeger Publishers, 2001), 28.
[81] "Memorandum on the discussion at the 312th meeting of the

National Security Council, Washington, February 7, 1957," US Department of State, https://history.state.gov/historicaldocuments/frus1955-57v19/d108.

[82] General Maxwell D. Taylor, "Evaluation of the Effect on US Operational Plans of Soviet Army Equipment Introduced Into Cuba," National Security Archives, November 2, 1962. Accessed September 22, 2015, http://nsarchive.gwu.edu/NSAEBB/NSAEBB397/docs/doc%2022%202011-2-62%20memo%20to%20JFK%20re%20invasion%20plans.pdf.

[83] Niall McCarthy, "The Biggest Military Budgets as a Percentage of GDP," *Forbes*, June 25, 2014, http://www.forbes.com/sites/niallmccarthy/2015/06/25/the-biggest-military-budgets-as-a-percentage-of-gdp-infographic-2/.

[84] Max Fisher, "Why Is the US OK with Israel Having Nuclear Weapons but Not Iran?," *The Washington Post*, December 2, 2013, https://www.washingtonpost.com/news/worldviews/wp/2013/12/02/why-is-the-u-s-okay-with-israel-having-nuclear-weapons-but-not-iran/.

[85] Memorandum, 349th meeting of the National Security Council, January 22, 1959, US Department of State, https://history.state.gov/historicaldocuments/frus1958-60v03/d47.

[86] Daniel Ellsberg, "US Nuclear War Planning for a Hundred Holocausts," Daniel Ellsberg's Website, September 13, 2009, http://www.ellsberg.net/archive/us-nuclear-war-planning-for-a-hundred-holocausts.

www.ingramcontent.com/pod-product-compliance
Lightning Source LLC
Chambersburg PA
CBHW072202280526
45788CB00002B/845